BU✝LT
TO
LEAD

BUILT TO LEAD

TO

LEAD

Forged by Purpose.
Fueled by Faith.

KYLE MCGEE

Published by Best Seller Publishing®, St. Augustine, FL
Best Seller Publishing® is a registered trademark.
Printed in the United States of America.

ISBN: 978-1-969338-58-8

This publication is designed to provide accurate and authoritative information with regard to the subject matter covered. It is sold with the understanding that the publisher is not engaged in rendering legal, accounting, or other professional advice. If legal advice or other expert assistance is required, the services of a competent professional should be sought. The opinions expressed by the author in this book are not endorsed by Best Seller Publishing® and are the sole responsibility of the author rendering the opinion.

For more information, please write:
Best Seller Publishing®
1775 US-1 #1070
St. Augustine, FL 32084
or call 1 (626) 765-9750

Visit us online at: www.BestSellerPublishing.org

DEDICATION

To my wife, Peyton—for your unwavering support, steadfast belief in me, and the grace with which you guide and nurture our children. I would not be half the man I am today without you by my side.

To my boys, Clark, Camden, and Brooks—for the joy, laughter, and purpose you bring to my life. You remind me daily of what truly matters and inspire me to keep building a legacy worth leaving.

To my parents—for raising me with faith at the center, instilling in me the value of hard work, and teaching me to treat people with respect. I am deeply grateful for your example of what it means to be both a present parent and a steady guide. Because of you, I have a model worth striving to emulate every day.

TABLE OF CONTENTS

FOREWORD

It's an honor to write the foreword for *Built to Lead*. Not because I've known Kyle for years—but because of what this book stands for.

This is a book about real leadership. Not the Instagram version. Not the title-chasing, spotlight-hungry kind. The kind that's built quietly—through character, consistency, and faith.

Kyle doesn't preach at you; he speaks to you.

He's honest about failure, humble about success, and bold about what truly matters. That's rare.

And it's exactly what this world needs right now.

We're living in a time where people confuse attention with impact. But real leadership has nothing to do with followers or status. It's about influence—earned through integrity, humility, and service.

It's about showing up when it's inconvenient, doing what's right when it's unpopular, and taking responsibility when others run from it.

That's the heartbeat of this book. It's a reminder that leadership is not a position; it's a calling.

It's not about being in charge; it's about being entrusted. And it starts long before anyone else notices.

I was raised in a family of faith. My parents taught me early that everything we have is a gift from God and that leadership is stewardship. Now, 24 years into marriage and raising five incredible kids of my own, I see that truth more clearly than ever.

God's blessed my family in ways I could've never earned, and my greatest calling is to lead them well.That's why this message hits home.

Because *Built to Lead* isn't just about business or influence. It's about living and leading in a way that honors God, strengthens families, and multiplies impact.

Every chapter challenges you to go deeper. To grow stronger. To stop waiting for the "perfect time" and start leading where you are.

If you want to build a life that matters, read this book. If you want to lead with purpose instead of ego, study it. If you want to become the kind of person others can count on, live it.

Because the truth is, you don't need a bigger platform to lead. You just need the courage to go first.

That's what this book will help you do.

— Chad Willardson

Founder, Pacific Capital and ELEVATED
6x Bestselling Author of *Fully Invested and Smart, Not Spoiled*
Husband to Amber, and proud dad of five

INTRODUCTION

It was February 6, 2016, in Key West, Florida.

Two months post-college graduation and living in a new city, I would have my first of many signs that it was time for something to change. I was isolated, without any family or friends nearby, and was leaning on alcohol for a good time.

One month into this new life, I woke up in a jail cell.

If you've never had that experience, I pray you never do. I had no idea how I got there or what I had done. At 21 years old, I found myself in solitary confinement, terrified, ashamed, and wondering how my life had spiraled so quickly. That night, I had made reckless choices and got behind the wheel of my truck completely blacked out—too many shots, too many bad decisions, and by God's grace alone, I didn't hurt myself or someone else. I blew a 0.251, over three times the legal blood alcohol content limit.

You'd think that moment would've straightened me out. It didn't. Even after my dad drove 14 hours to be with me after the incident, even after I promised myself I'd change, I continued down the path of reckless partying and self-destruction.

Two years later—almost to the day, February 8, 2018—I lost my hero and best friend, my father, to a short six-month battle with cancer. His dying wish for me was simple: *Stop abusing alcohol.* And yet, even then, I didn't change.

It wasn't until God used the steadfast love of my wife, Peyton, and my own breaking point that I finally surrendered. I realized I could not outrun God's plan for my life. Through my faith and the support of those who refused to give up on me, I began to rebuild: slowly, imperfectly, but intentionally.

Now, years later, I'm the husband of an incredible woman, the father of three beautiful boys, and the leader of multiple thriving businesses. Together with my team, I've built Sunchase Companies, a very strong real estate development and investment company that has built and sold over 120 homes, developed over $30 million worth of projects, and currently operates eight apartment communities totaling 314 units.

But here's the truth: I'm not special. I've made plenty of mistakes. I'm not "naturally gifted." I'm just a man who surrendered and committed to take daily action and learn what it takes to lead.

And that's why I'm writing this book.

There was no lightning-bolt moment. No divine memo that showed up on my doorstep. Just a persistent whisper that wouldn't go away.

At first, I tried to dismiss it. After all, there are over 50,000 books on Amazon with the word *leadership* in the title. Who was I to believe the world needed mine? What could I possibly say that hadn't already been said, probably better, by someone older, smarter, more experienced? But the longer I resisted, the louder that whisper became.

I've said for years that I would write a book "someday." But someday kept getting pushed further down the road. The final kick in the butt for me to actually take the leap and put pen to paper came when I lost my mother-in-law, Janie Clark, to an 18-month battle with cancer. She was only 57 years old. My dad was 52 years old when he lost his battle to cancer. Those were incredibly hard seasons—ones I would never wish on anyone—but they also opened my eyes to the fragility of life and the lie of "someday."

The truth is, we aren't guaranteed anything, not even tomorrow. And I made a decision: I will not stand idle on my goals. I will take massive, inspired daily action toward the things God has placed in my heart to do. Writing this book is one of them.

Once I had personally committed to writing this book, the true test came: telling my wife. It was early on a Tuesday morning. Coffee was in my hand, and I was still half asleep when I looked at Peyton and said, "I'm going to write a book on leadership and have it completed by the end of this year."

She raised her eyebrows, smiled, and asked, "Do you have enough wisdom yet to write a book?"

She said it with love, but also with that knowing look only your spouse can give—the kind of look that slices through your ego and straight into your soul. I laughed because, honestly, she had a point.

Do I have enough wisdom to write a book? Maybe not. But I'm writing it anyway. Because this isn't a book about having all the answers. This is a book about the journey. It's about what I've learned about the qualities of great leaders so far, and what I'm still learning every single day as a husband, a father, a business owner, a community member, and most importantly, a follower of Jesus Christ.

This book is not a blueprint. I hope for you to see it as a set of building blocks. And at the foundation of it all is one unshakable belief:

You were made for this.

Not just the "natural" leaders. Not just the executives, pastors, entrepreneurs, or influencers. *You.* You were created with a purpose, placed in a specific time and place, surrounded by people only you can reach. That's not random. That's calling. Whether you're leading a business, a team, a family, a small group, a classroom, or simply yourself, this book is for you. You don't need a title to lead. You don't need permission. You don't need to wait until you feel ready.

You were built to lead.

WHY THIS BOOK? WHY NOW?

We are living in a leadership crisis.

Take a look at the world around us. Institutions we once trusted are crumbling. Mental health struggles are surging. Trust in leaders, systems, and even in one another is fading fast. The divorce rate is the highest it's ever been, and families are falling apart. Outside noise is deafening. Social media rewards outrage. The world is more connected than ever, yet we are more divided, disillusioned, and disoriented. Our culture incentivizes self-promotion over service.

Amid all this, it feels like everyone is waiting for someone else to step up and to speak truth, to take responsibility, to lead with clarity, humility, and courage. But here's the hard truth: The cavalry isn't coming. It's us. It's you.

We don't need more celebrities or influencers. We don't need more polished press releases or corporate jargon. We need everyday, ordinary people like you and me who understand that leadership is not reserved for a select few with titles or platforms. It's for anyone willing to own their impact and live anchored to something greater than themselves.

That "something greater" is found in Christ. More than ever, our society needs leaders who aren't swayed by public opinion, but are rooted in unshakable truth. *Faith-centered leadership isn't optional anymore. It's essential.*

It doesn't matter if you are leading a Fortune 500 company or a small startup, guiding a team, raising a family, mentoring a teenager, or building a marriage from the ground up. My hope is that this book lights a fire in your heart to seek God's wisdom and faithfully step up to the people and the places He has entrusted you to lead.

Because leadership isn't about charisma, control, or corner offices. It's not about having all the answers or being the loudest voice in the room. Leadership is about influence. It's about impact. It's about the legacy you leave through how you show up, how you serve, how you stand firm when the pressure rises and no one else will. Leadership is about doing what's right even when it's not popular. It's about seeing people, lifting them, calling out the gold in them, and calling them to more. It's about living with such consistency that people trust your voice because they've watched your actions.

This book isn't just a call to leadership. It's a call to responsibility. It's a call to become the kind of person others can follow not because you're perfect but because you're grounded, growing, and willing to go first.

THE FUNDAMENTALS THAT MATTER MOST

This book isn't a formula. It's not called *Ten Steps to Be a Great Leader* because leadership isn't a checklist you can breeze through on your lunch break.

This is a return to the fundamentals. The timeless, tested principles that real leaders build their lives on. Not flashy trends. Not personality hacks. Not leadership fads that fade in six months. Just the unshakable foundations that outlast seasons, industries, and circumstances.

We're going to break down the building blocks of effective leadership: vision, discipline, humility, communication, self-awareness, time management, decision-making, and legacy.

Not in a boardroom simulation. Not in a business school case study. In life. In the heat of conflict. In the quiet of personal battles. In the rhythms of work, family, faith, and calling. You'll hear from real people. Entrepreneurs building companies from scratch. Pastors shepherding communities through spiritual storms. Coaches molding character in young athletes. Parents navigating the sacred responsibility of raising the next generation. And everyday men and women, often unnoticed, leading with extraordinary conviction and courage where it matters most.

Because leadership doesn't always come with a platform. Sometimes it looks like staying when it would be easier to leave. Sometimes it looks like serving without credit, forgiving when it hurts, or making the tough call that no one will understand in the moment.

Leadership isn't one-size-fits-all, either. As you move through this book, you will see that leadership looks a little different on everyone. Some leaders are bold and outspoken, whereas others are quiet and consistent. But underneath it all, the roots are the same. Those roots are what this book is all about. With strong roots, fruit will come. Once the foundation is strong, the house can weather any storm.

BUILT THROUGH FIRE

Every great leader I've ever met, whether on a stage, in the boardroom, or behind the scenes, has one thing in common: They've been through fire.

They've been tested. They've been stretched. They've walked through hell and kept going. They've faced rejection that stung deeper than they'd admit. Betrayal from people they trusted. Doubt that crept in during the quiet hours when no one was watching. Burnout that left them wondering if they could keep going. They've made the hard calls, carried the weight, and stood alone when everyone else sat down.

These aren't the highlight reel moments. These are the scars behind the stage. The real stories behind the leadership titles and polished bios. But here's the truth: those fires didn't destroy them. They forged them. Leadership isn't found; it's made. It's not handed out in an award ceremony or earned through a résumé. It's forged in the private battles, in the pressure, in the heat of real-life situations where you want to tap out but choose to press on instead.

I know this because I've been there.

In late 2022, I was leading a small real estate team of seven as interest rates climbed and the housing market shifted. One morning, in our weekly meeting, I told my team we were going to slow down our new starts. I've always prided myself on being transparent, but the second the words left my mouth, the room shifted. Almost in unison, my team turned with the same question written on their faces: *Is my job safe?*

I reassured them. Everyone's job was safe. We'd adapt. We'd figure it out together. You could feel the relief.

But later that afternoon, when I sat down with my business partners, reality hit like a ton of bricks. We had millions of dollars in unsold inventory and no certainty about the economy. My partners didn't just want to slow down construction—they didn't want to start any new homes at all. I realized that the only way to keep my people, especially our superintendents, was to keep building. I told my partners I didn't want to let anyone go and even shared the conversation I'd had with the team that morning.

One partner looked at me and said words that cut deep: "This is the hard part about business and being the guy that has to make the tough decisions."

Less than 24 hours after assuring my team their jobs were safe, I had to go back and have two of the hardest conversations of my career.

That was just one of the many fires I've been through. And here's what it taught me: Leadership isn't about never being rattled. It's about not letting the rattling shake your identity. You are not your circumstances. You are your response.

The furnace is where clarity comes. The fire strips away the ego. It purifies your motives. It shows you what matters most and what never did.

In these pages, I'm not giving you a blueprint from the mountaintop. I'm inviting you into the trenches. I'll share moments that shaped me; some I'm proud of, while others I've wrestled to make peace with. I'll tell you about the failures, the pivots, the unexpected wins, and the silent breakthroughs that nobody saw coming.

You'll also hear the stories of other leaders who've been through their own fires, emerged refined, and now lead with humility and courage.

Some of what you read might challenge you. Good. Growth doesn't happen in comfort. You've heard the phrase "Get comfortable being uncomfortable." But there comes a time when you stop hearing it and start living it. That time is now.

Here's my promise: If you lean in and engage with this book, wrestle with the ideas, apply the principles, and take ownership of your leadership journey, you will not walk away the same. You may walk away scarred. You may walk away humbled. But you'll definitely walk away stronger, more grounded, more confident, and more refined.

Because the fire doesn't just expose the leader in you. It builds you into one.

LEADERSHIP IS INFLUENCE, NOT POSITION

If you want to find real leadership, don't look at who's in charge. Look at who's making a difference.

I've seen entry-level employees lead up the chain of command by consistently bringing solutions, taking ownership, and treating their work with excellence. I've watched single moms lead their households with more clarity, courage, and conviction than some CEOs with sprawling org charts and corner offices. I've seen quiet, behind-the-scenes servants shift the culture of an entire organization, not because they were loud or in control, but because their character was magnetic and their example impossible to ignore.

That's because leadership is not about position; it's about influence. And influence doesn't require a title. It doesn't require permission. It doesn't wait for someone to hand it a microphone or a nameplate or a promotion.

Influence begins with trust. And trust is built through character, consistency, and the willingness to go first.

Go first in honesty. Go first in responsibility. Go first in vulnerability, in accountability, in generosity, in forgiveness, and in truth.

I am a huge quote junkie, as you'll see if you stick with me through the rest of this book (And if you do, God bless you)...

One of my favorite quotes of all time was made famous by John F. Kennedy:

"A rising tide lifts all boats."

Great leaders are rising tides. Their influence doesn't just help themselves; it also serves to lift the people around them. It elevates the room. It changes the temperature of a conversation, the tone of a meeting, the trajectory of a team. Their presence creates possibilities for others. That's leadership. And it has nothing to do with job titles or salary bands or how many people report to you.

By the end, my hope is that you'll walk away with clarity and conviction about what leadership truly is and how *you* were uniquely built to embody it. Wherever God has placed you, you can lead with boldness. Not someday. Not when things are perfect. Now.

PART ONE
THE FOUNDATIONS
OF LEADERSHIP

CHAPTER 1

WHAT IS LEADERSHIP, REALLY?

If your actions inspire others to dream more,
learn more, do more, and become more, you are
a leader.

—JOHN QUINCY ADAMS

In John 13, just before His crucifixion, Jesus did something astonishing. He wrapped a towel around His waist, filled a basin with water, and began washing His disciples' feet. This was not a symbolic act or a staged performance. It was real, raw humility. In the ancient world, washing feet was seen as a dirty task that was reserved for those on the bottom rung of the household hierarchy.

And yet, here was the King of Kings on His knees, serving His followers.

After finishing, Jesus said to them, "Do you understand what I have done for you? ... You call me 'Teacher' and 'Lord,' and rightly so, for that is what I am. Now that I, your Lord and Teacher, have washed your feet, you also should wash one another's feet. I have set you an example that you should do as I have done for you" (John 13:12–15 NIV). He continues: "Very truly I tell you, no servant is greater than his master, nor is a messenger greater than the one who sent him. Now that you know these things, you will be blessed if you do them" (verses 16–17 NIV).

With this moment, He redefined greatness. He showed that true leadership isn't about privilege or position. It's about serving those who are around us. He didn't diminish His authority through this act; He amplified it. He modeled a love so powerful and a humility so rare that it pierced the hearts of those who followed Him.

That's what leadership looks like in its purest form: *selfless, sacrificial, and stunningly human.*

LEADERSHIP IS A RESPONSIBILITY

Far too often, leadership gets reduced to roles, titles, or charisma. Contrary to that belief, leadership is often not about your position or title but about your posture.

Leadership is a sacred responsibility. It's about recognizing the influence you carry and stewarding it well. That influence might be in a classroom, a conference room, a kitchen, or a construction site. Regardless of where it is, it's important to recognize that it's not about being in charge; it's about being entrusted.

The weight of leadership doesn't come from the scope of your reach—it comes from the *depth of your impact.*

And impact always begins with integrity.

The truest form of leadership often happens in the mundane. It happens in the way you show up for your spouse when you're tired. In how you respond when you're overlooked. In what you do when no one's watching.

One life, fully lived with integrity, can shape generations. And that is why leadership is a responsibility.

AUTHENTIC LEADERSHIP: THE POWER OF BEING REAL

I've always been drawn to learning from great leaders, and what stands out to me is how different they can be. Some lead with quiet strength, whereas others light up a room the moment they walk in. Some wear suits, others steel-toed boots. A few are fast-paced and full of energy, but others are reserved and choose their words carefully. Despite these differences, the common thread among the leaders I admire most is their authenticity.

True leaders don't put on a performance; they show up as themselves. They're not obsessed with appearing competent; they're committed to being trustworthy. They strive to foster connection and communication with those around them in a way that feels natural. And I don't know about you, but I can always feel when someone is trying too hard to be someone they're not. It's almost cringe-worthy. Time after time, authenticity speaks louder than charisma.

A perfect example of this is found in two giants of business: Sam Walton and Jeff Bezos. On the surface, they couldn't have been more different.

Sam Walton was warm, down-to-earth, and deeply relational. He didn't lead with ego; he led with empathy. Even with immense wealth, he chose simplicity—driving his old truck, walking the Wal-Mart store aisles, and shaking hands with employees. He built trust by showing he cared. We will explore more of his story later in this book.

Jeff Bezos, on the other hand, led with clarity and vision. He was intense and demanding. He had high standards and drove innovation with precision. He wasn't warm in the traditional sense, but he was unwaveringly focused. His influence was born not from likability but from strategic foresight.

Here's the point: both men were leaders. Both were wildly successful. Both were authentic. They didn't try to copy each other or mold themselves into what the world expected. They led from the core of who they were. That's the power of authenticity. It frees you to lead in a way that is congruent with your convictions, not someone else's personality.

POWER VS. INFLUENCE: THE FORK IN THE ROAD

Power and influence tend to be used interchangeably, but they lead to very different destinations.

Power is positional. It's granted by others, can easily be taken away, works through hierarchy, and demands compliance. It's external.

Influence is personal. It's earned over time, it inspires commitment, and it is rooted in trust. It's internal.

Power can control behavior and is often dictatorial. Real influence can shape belief and inspires people to follow because they believe in where the journey is going.

Jesus could have ruled with power—He had all the authority. Instead, He chose to lead with influence. He invited people into transformation, never forcing it upon them. The greatest leaders in history, from Lincoln to Mandela, chose influence over dominance. They knew that although power creates momentary movement, influence can create *lasting change.*

THE MYTH OF THE "NATURAL" LEADER

It's a compelling story.

It is easy to fall into the idea that some people are just *born* leaders. They have charisma in their DNA. They seem to glide through life two steps ahead of everyone else. They walk into a room and immediately take command. They speak, and people lean in. They lead because, well, that's just who they are.

It's also a dangerous idea.

Because when we buy into the myth of the "natural leader," we automatically disqualify ourselves if we don't see those traits in the mirror. We tell ourselves, *I'm not bold enough, not confident enough, not gifted enough.* And so we shrink back. We play small. We wait for someone else to lead.

I know this mindset intimately because I've lived it.

Ironically, I was the captain of my sports teams growing up. Even now, some of my friends still jokingly call me "Captain," like it's permanently stitched onto my identity. From the outside, I checked the boxes: I was the guy people looked to. I went out for the coin toss, was never shy to speak up, and always had the coach's ear.

But what people didn't see was the battle happening inside.

As a kid—and even now, as a grown man—I've wrestled with doubt. I've questioned my decisions. I've failed hard and often. I've made mistakes that cost me trust, time, and relationships. And I've had to learn (usually the hard way) how to own them, learn from them, and keep leading anyway.

So if leadership were something you're just *born with*, I would've been disqualified long ago.

But what I've come to realize through years of building businesses, leading teams, mentoring young leaders, and navigating seasons of personal failure and growth is this:

Leadership isn't just a natural talent. It's a skill. A muscle.

And just like any muscle, it can be strengthened—with time, pressure, and intentional repetition.

You want to know how I know that's true? Because I'm not the same leader today that I was ten years ago. Not even close. If leadership was something you were either born with or without, I would have peaked in high school, and that would have been a tragedy. Instead, leadership has become something I've learned through trial and error, through wins and wounds. I've grown by reading books, yes—but more importantly, by taking action and living out the principles in real life: in boardrooms, job sites, coffee shops, and within my home. And that's good news. That's *really* good news. Because it means leadership isn't reserved for the elite. It's not about being the loudest voice or the flashiest personality. It's not a club you're born into. It is about working at it a little bit every day until you eventually grow into the leader you were meant to be.

Leadership is a calling available to anyone willing to answer it.

Whether you're a high school student or a CEO, a stay-at-home parent or a solopreneur, a church volunteer or a construction foreman, you can lead. You *are* leading. The question is whether you'll step fully into that identity and intentionally develop the muscles that leadership requires. And if you're willing to do the work, then leadership will no longer be something you admire in others. It'll be something you live out in your own life.

God doesn't expect you to be born ready. He equips those who step forward in faith.

As 2 Timothy 1:7 (NIV) reminds us, "For the Spirit God gave us does not make us timid, but gives us power, love and self-discipline."

That's the leadership toolkit right there. The power to act, a love to serve, and the discipline to keep growing.

THE RIPPLE EFFECT IS REAL

Never underestimate the ripple effect of your daily decisions.

When you lead with integrity in a situation where cutting corners would be easier, you're creating ripples. When you honor someone's presence with full attention instead of multitasking, you're creating ripples. When you call someone higher instead of letting them coast, you're creating ripples. That kind of influence may not show up on an org chart, but it's shaping hearts, cultures, and outcomes in ways most people never see.

Think of a stone dropped into a still pond. The circles move outward, far beyond the point of impact. That's how influence works. One moment of courage or kindness or clarity can send waves into someone's future. You may never know how far they'll go.

And that's the challenge: to stop thinking about leadership in terms of spotlight and status, and start thinking about it in terms of responsibility and ripple.

Because the real leaders in this world? They're the ones who wake up each day asking not "How can I get ahead?" but "Who can I lift today?"

You Don't Need a Title; You Need Courage

If leadership were just about position, it'd be easy. We'd wait until we were promoted. We'd wait until someone gave us authority. We'd wait for the green light from someone higher up the ladder. But real leadership doesn't wait.

Leadership requires courage: the courage to act before the spotlight hits, to serve when no one's watching, and to believe that your influence matters even when your résumé is still a work in progress. And let me say this as clearly as I can: Age does not determine leadership. You don't need to hit 40 before your voice counts. You don't need gray hair, decades of experience, or a long list of accolades to step up and lead. What you need is vision. What you need is courage.

I know this because I've lived it.

When I was in my early 20s, I became the youngest board member of a local charity organization. To be honest, I was honored to be invited, but I was also intimidated. The other members were older, more accomplished, and far more connected. They had titles. They had reputations. I had a lot to learn. But early on, I made a decision. I've never been one to sit on the sidelines. I might not have had the years, but I had the energy. I had ideas. And I wasn't going to waste my seat at the table.

So I spoke up.

Not to hear myself talk, but to bring fresh solutions to stale problems. I listened carefully to what wasn't being said, and when I felt a conviction, I shared it respectfully but confidently. I came with ideas, yes, but more importantly, I followed through with action. I didn't just suggest new initiatives; I volunteered to lead them. I rolled up my sleeves, made calls, pulled together teams, and made things happen.

And something interesting started to shift. The very people I'd admired began to look up to me. Not because of my age, but because of my ownership. Not because I was the most experienced, but because I was consistent. Because I showed up. Because I took action. That experience taught me something I've never forgotten:

Leadership is earned through courage, not chronology.

I've seen teenagers lead their peers with strength and conviction. I've seen interns rally teams through attitude and work ethic. I've seen stay-at-home parents build movements from their kitchen tables. Leadership doesn't wait for permission. It starts with the question, "What can I do with what I have, where I am?" and then, it answers that question with action.

You don't need a title to lead.

- You need **courage** to step out of your comfort zone and stick your neck out there.
- You need the **humility** to admit when you're wrong, even when you're the youngest in the room.
- You need the **discipline** to follow through when everyone else is letting things slide.
- You need the **grit** to stay engaged and keep showing up— even when you feel like an outsider, even when you're underestimated.
- You need the **conviction** to speak up for what matters, even if your voice shakes. Even if your idea doesn't get picked. Even if no one notices—yet.
- And you need the **faith** to believe that doing the right thing, consistently, with integrity and love, will multiply your influence over time.

Because courage is contagious. When one person dares to lead with character, it gives others permission to do the same. One act of courage—especially when it's unexpected—can unlock a chain reaction of leadership.

And it all begins the moment you stop waiting to be chosen and start living like you've already been called.

YOU WERE BUILT TO LEAD

Leadership is for the *equipped*. And I've got good news for you. God has equipped you.

You were not created to shrink back. You were made to step forward.

You were not built for fear—you were built for faith.

You don't need a platform to make a difference—just *purpose* and *presence*.

So wherever God has placed you—your home, your church, your company, or your community—STEP UP AND LEAD! Not with a crown, but with a big heart. Not with dominance, but with direction. Not to be impressive, but to make an impact.

Jesus showed us that leadership is love in motion.

Now it's your turn.

Key Highlights

- True leadership isn't about status or authority but about serving others, even when it's uncomfortable or unseen.
- Great leaders come in many forms—quiet or bold, relational or visionary. What unites them is authenticity—leading from their true self, not trying to imitate others or perform for approval.
- The "natural leader" myth is damaging—it makes people disqualify themselves.
- Leadership is a developable skill, like a muscle, built through practice, failure, integrity, and persistence.
- Leadership doesn't require permission, age, or status—it requires courage to act, integrity to stay consistent, and faith to keep going.
- Real leaders rise by stepping up with what they have, right where they are.

Reflection Questions

1. What story am I telling with my actions each day? What kind of example am I setting?
2. What's one small, consistent act of leadership I can begin practicing this week—at home, at work, or in my community?
3. Am I living in such a way that others would want to follow—not because they have to, but because they trust and respect me?

CHAPTER 2

Vision—Seeing Beyond the Now

Where there is no vision, the people perish.

—Proverbs 29:18 KJV

A leader is one who knows the way,
goes the way, and shows the way.

—John Maxwell

The Power of Vision

Vision is the cornerstone of effective leadership because it defines the destination and fuels the journey. Without vision, leadership defaults to management and is focused on maintaining the status quo rather than moving toward something greater. Vision gives leadership purpose beyond tasks and meaning beyond metrics. It allows leaders to chart a course, anticipate challenges, and inspire their people with a sense of hope and direction. A clear and compelling vision aligns decision-making, energizes teams, and creates unity of purpose. It transforms a group of individuals into a mission-driven movement.

Vision also gives the leader staying power—something to hold onto when adversity hits. It's what keeps you anchored in your "why" when the "how" gets hard. Simply put, you cannot lead people somewhere you haven't already seen in your spirit. And if you can't see it, they won't either. Vision isn't just a leadership tool—it *is* leadership. It's the difference between wandering and building, between surviving and leaving a legacy.

In the early years of my business journey, I struggled with one of the most important responsibilities of leadership: casting vision. I had it all written down—bold, exciting, and full of possibility—but I kept it to myself. Why? Because it felt too big, too ambitious, and frankly, I had no idea how we were going to get there. I feared that if I shared it, people would think I was naive or delusional. So I stayed quiet. And that silence came at a cost. Without vision, my team had no true north. We drifted. We dabbled in different directions, wore ourselves thin, and never achieved excellence in any one area. We were good at a lot, but great at nothing.

The turning point came when I decided to share the vision. And to my surprise, the team didn't laugh. They didn't blink. They leaned in. And in that moment, everything began to change. Speaking the vision out loud not only clarified it for them—it clarified it for me. I had to give language to what was previously just a fuzzy idea in my head. That process forced me to crystallize my thoughts and make the vision real. The team rallied behind it. They were motivated, aligned, and energized. And for the first time, we began moving in the same direction with intentionality and focus.

WORLD-CHANGING VISION

One of the most striking examples of divine vision is found in the Old Testament story of Nehemiah. Living in exile, Nehemiah heard that the walls of Jerusalem (his ancestral home) lay in ruins. His heart was broken, and he wept. But he didn't stop there. He prayed, fasted, and asked God for favor. And in time, a vision was birthed in his spirit: to return to Jerusalem and rebuild the walls.

It's important to note that Nehemiah wasn't a priest or a prophet. He was a cupbearer—a servant in the king's palace. By worldly standards, he wasn't qualified to lead a massive construction project. But God had given him a vision, and that vision stirred him to action. When he shared it with others, the people responded: "Let us rise up and build" (Nehemiah 2:18 KJV). What followed was a remarkable display of unity, leadership, and perseverance. Despite external threats, internal doubt, and overwhelming odds, Nehemiah rallied the people and rebuilt the wall in just 52 days.

His story is a reminder that vision starts in the spirit before it's ever seen with the eyes. It comes through prayer, burden, and a deep sense of calling. Nehemiah's vision didn't begin with strategy; it began with surrender. He sought God first, trusted in His provision, and then, boldly cast the vision God gave him. That's what made the people rally. That's what made the mission succeed. Nehemiah didn't just rebuild a wall—he rebuilt the hope of a nation. His story shows us that when vision is God-breathed and leader-owned, even the most broken things can be restored.

In his book *Visioneering*, Andy Stanley puts it this way: "Vision is a mental picture of what could be, fueled by a passion that it should be." I love that. It reminds us that vision isn't just a business buzzword; it's a sacred stewardship. Great leaders throughout history have understood this. Martin Luther King Jr.'s "I Have a Dream" speech didn't just describe a preferred future; it sparked a movement. Walt Disney imagined a world of wonder before a single ride was built. Steve Jobs saw a world transformed by technology before the iPhone was even an idea. These visionaries weren't just dreamers—they were builders of the future. They saw beyond the now and invited others to help make that vision a reality.

Vision in Action

One of the most inspiring visionary leaders I've had the distinct pleasure of working very closely with is Robert Rinke in Pensacola Beach, Florida. Robert is the definition of a visionary, and the story he shared on my podcast *Legacy Builders with Kyle McGee* (Episode 14, for those interested) of how Portofino Island Resort came to fruition is worth repeating.

Where most people saw 40 windswept acres at the end of Pensacola Beach, Robert Rinke saw a lifestyle people would enjoy for generations. Before a single shovel hit sand, he spent late nights at Barnes & Noble studying resort towns and amenities, and then, he wrote a 12-page vision plan organized around "lifestyle, health, fitness, relaxation, recreation, and adventure."

Armed with that plan, he took a 15-minute meeting with his business partner and the land owner at the time, Fred Levin, and nailed it. Levin greenlit the concept and told him to "hire the best architect money can buy" for resort condos. Rinke set up a true design charrette, flying in top firms and even paying two finalists $60,000 each to compete; four days of iterate-present-iterate, until a clear design emerged.

The land planner proposed an unconventional triangular tower footprint a "football-field apart," so seven of nine condos on each floor could see both the Gulf and the bay. That bold geometric decision doubled glass exposure over typical condos, transforming view corridors into a daily experience.

Then came the resistance. A well-funded group sued to stop Portofino. Paradoxically, the delay became a gift. Demand stayed strong, interest rates fell ~2 percent, values on the beach surged, and, most importantly, Rinke used the time to refine floorplans, amenities, and one massive pivot: ditching exterior insulation finishing system (EFIS)/steel-stud exterior walls for an all-concrete envelope.

He convened the structural engineer, architect, and a water-intrusion consultant. The verdict: EFIS stucco could meet code but was vulnerable to long-term infiltration; concrete would be heavier and ~10 percent more expensive (≈$3.5 million more, then) but far more resilient on a hurricane coastline. They chose concrete—and it became Portofino's number-one selling feature for owners who wanted to "lock the door" and come back to an intact building.

This is what vision-led leadership does: It sees beyond the now—beyond lawsuits, budget pressure, and status-quo methods—and designs for the future you're promising people. Rinke didn't sell "units." He sold a way of life, and then, engineered the building to match the promise.

Today, Portofino is the most distinguishable property on Pensacola Beach and is a destination people all over the world come to enjoy on a regular basis.

That is what Nehemiah's energy is all about: Start with the burden and the picture in your spirit, and then, organize people, plans, and materials to make it real. And when opposition comes, let it refine the vision rather than shrink it.

Why Vision Matters for Leadership

Vision is not optional for a leader—it's essential. It is the very foundation of inspired action. A strong vision provides clarity, direction, and purpose. It paints a compelling picture of the future that pulls people forward and breathes life into their daily efforts. It aligns resources, ignites passion, and gives meaning to the grind. But vision alone is not enough—it has to be shared, believed in, and embodied by the right people. When you build a team of "A" Players—high-capacity individuals who share your core values and fully buy into the mission—anything becomes possible. When those people are rowing in the same direction, the momentum becomes unstoppable. That's the power of alignment. You move from merely working on tasks to building something of significance. With a unified team, even the most audacious vision moves from improbable to inevitable. The synergy created by a group of high-character, purpose-driven people rallying around a clear and compelling vision is one of the most powerful forces in leadership.

THE POWER OF ALIGNMENT

One of the most common traps leaders fall into is setting a vision that's too small, too safe, or too easily attainable. It feels comfortable to aim for what's realistic—what can be achieved with current resources, skills, or systems. But that kind of vision won't inspire anyone, including you. A true vision lives on the fringe—just out of reach of what seems possible. And that's exactly where it should be. Why? Because a big vision stretches you. It forces you to grow as a leader, to develop new capacities, to get creative, and to become someone you're not yet. As you rise to the challenge, you'll naturally lift others with you. That brings us back to one of my favorite quotes: "A rising tide lifts all boats." When you set a bold, faith-filled vision, it pulls the best out of your team. It demands excellence, collaboration, and commitment. It transforms not only what you achieve but also who you all become in the process. A safe vision is maintained. A bold vision multiplies.

A powerful example of bold vision creating alignment and transformation comes from Sara Blakely, the founder of Spanx.

Blakely didn't come from a business background. She was selling fax machines door-to-door when she had the idea for footless pantyhose. It was a simple problem she wanted to solve for herself—smooth lines under white trousers—but the vision she carried for the solution wasn't small. She didn't just want to make a new undergarment. She wanted to disrupt an entire industry, empower women to feel confident in their own skin, and build a brand that celebrated real bodies and real voices.

From the beginning, her vision lived on the fringe. She had no connections, no investors, and no experience in fashion. But she believed so strongly in the outcome that she poured her life savings into the idea, pitched it relentlessly, and brought people around her who caught the vision too. She wasn't just selling a product; she was inviting people to be part of a movement.

That bold, purpose-driven vision attracted top talent, loyal customers, and eventually major retailers. When Oprah endorsed Spanx as one of her favorite things, the momentum exploded. But what truly sustained the company's growth was the alignment around Blakely's mission. Her team didn't just work for Spanx—they *believed* in Spanx. And that belief showed up in everything from product design to company culture.

Years later, when she sold a majority stake in Spanx for $1.2 billion, she didn't just celebrate alone. She gave every employee $10,000 and two first-class plane tickets to anywhere in the world—a gesture that perfectly embodied her original vision: bold, generous, and people-first.

Sara Blakely's story reminds us that big, daring vision doesn't require perfect credentials, just relentless belief and the courage to go first. Her persistence mirrors the biblical truth that vision requires perseverance and faith when the outcome is unseen. When a leader stretches beyond what's safe, they draw out the best in others too. That's the power of alignment through bold vision.

MAKE VISION CONTAGIOUS

Vision, when communicated with clarity and conviction, becomes contagious. It's not enough for a leader to simply have vision; it must be shared in a way that stirs hearts and moves people to action. Contagious vision is emotionally compelling—it speaks to something deeper than profit or performance. It taps into purpose. People want to be part of something bigger than themselves, and when a leader boldly articulates a future worth pursuing, it awakens that desire.

But a contagious vision also requires consistency. It has to be repeated often, reinforced through decisions, modeled in behavior, and celebrated in progress. When people see their leader fully bought in, they catch it. It spreads. It becomes embedded in the culture, guiding how people think, work, and show up every day. In time, the vision no longer belongs to just the leader—it becomes *everyone's* vision. And that's when the mission gains unstoppable momentum.

One of the most powerful examples of contagious vision in leadership comes from the world of professional football and from a man known more for his quiet conviction than for fiery speeches: Tony Dungy.

When Dungy took over the struggling Tampa Bay Buccaneers in 1996, the franchise was the laughingstock of the NFL. The team had a history of losing seasons, a toxic culture, and little hope. But Dungy came in with a clear, compelling vision—not just for winning games, but for transforming the entire culture from the inside out. He cast a vision of excellence, discipline, and integrity. And he refused to compromise.

What made Dungy's vision contagious wasn't his volume—it was his consistency. He modeled everything he preached. He was the same man in the locker room as he was in front of the cameras. He didn't scream. He didn't shame. He led by example, and it inspired deep loyalty. Players began to buy in—not just to the plays, but to the purpose behind them.

His vision for what a football program *could* be didn't stop in Tampa Bay. When he later became head coach of the Indianapolis Colts, he took the same contagious vision with him. He focused on character, accountability, and building men as much as athletes. That vision didn't just win games—it changed lives. And eventually, it led to a Super Bowl victory in 2007, making Dungy the first Black head coach to win an NFL championship.

Ask any of his players, and they'll tell you: Coach Dungy didn't just give them a game plan—he gave them a higher standard. His vision became *their* vision. And that's when everything changed. His consistent, humble leadership reflected Jesus's model in John 13, leading by example, not force.

THE DANGER OF WEAK OR ABSENT VISION

On the other hand, a weak vision is vague, uninspiring, and disconnected from reality. It sounds good but doesn't move people. It lacks both weight and direction, and without clarity, people will default to survival mode—reacting, drifting, and settling for mediocrity.

The absence of vision is dangerous. When people don't know where they're going, they become disoriented. In an organization, that shows up as burnout, confusion, misalignment, and stagnation. People start to work in silos, chase their own agendas, or simply clock in and out without passion or purpose. As leaders, we can't afford to let that happen. If we fail to cast a clear and compelling vision, we forfeit our right to lead. Vision is what makes the difference between managing and leading. Managers maintain. Leaders inspire.

One of the clearest cautionary tales of weak vision in the business world is the story of the photography brand Kodak.

For most of the twentieth century, Kodak was synonymous with photography. They dominated the film and camera market and had built a globally trusted brand. But in the 1980s and 1990s, as digital photography began to emerge, Kodak failed to see beyond the now. Ironically, they had invented one of the first digital cameras in 1975—but chose not to pursue it, fearing it would cannibalize their profitable film business.

Rather than reimagining their future and pivoting toward innovation, Kodak clung to what had worked in the past. Their leadership lacked the vision and courage to redefine the company's mission in the face of change. They became stuck in a maintenance mindset, managing decline instead of leading transformation.

As the industry shifted around them, Kodak's teams were left without a compelling direction. Innovation slowed. Energy faded. And by the time they tried to catch up, it was too late. In 2012, Kodak filed for bankruptcy, a shell of the industry leader it once was.

This is what happens when leaders protect the past instead of envisioning the future. Kodak didn't fail because they lacked resources or talent. They failed because they lacked vision. And without vision, even great organizations lose their way.

WHAT DO YOU WANT ME TO DO FOR YOU?

In Mark 10:51, Jesus asks a blind man a question that on the surface feels unnecessary:

"What do you want me to do for you?"

The man is blind. The answer seems obvious. Yet Jesus, the all-knowing Son of God, still asks. Why? Because vision starts with desire. Clarity begins with honesty. And prayer begins with specificity.

There is a deep and holy invitation buried in this question. Jesus isn't asking because He doesn't know. He's asking because He wants us to know—to name it, to own it, to believe that our desires matter to God.

If you're struggling with vision right now—unsure of where your life is headed, unclear on your next steps, stuck between purpose and confusion—start here:

Imagine you encounter Jesus on the street tomorrow. He looks you in the eyes. You can feel the love in His gaze. And then, He asks:

"What do you want me to do for you?"

How would you answer? Stop reading and really take a moment to think deeply about this question. Don't shrink it down to what you think is "realistic" or "appropriate." Let it be raw. Let it be real. Let it come from that deep, God-breathed part of your soul that still dares to hope.

However you answered that question is the seed of vision. It's not a business plan yet. It's not a strategy. It's not a five-year roadmap. But it's something far more important: It's *yours*.

Each of us was created with a distinct call on our lives. Not a copy-paste existence. Not a recycled dream. Something completely unique. A divine blueprint stitched into our souls before we were born (Psalm 139:16). And vision is how we begin to walk it out.

VISION STARTS WITH A QUESTION

Jesus knew the man was blind—but He also knew that he had to *want* to see. He had to say it out loud. The same is true for you and me. Clarity is often waiting on our honesty.

What do you want? What do you long for? What burns inside you that you've maybe been too scared to speak?

Let the Holy Spirit search your heart. Write it down. Speak it aloud. Pray it boldly. This is the starting point of vision—not just seeing something *out there*, but awakening something *in here*.

VISION IS PERSONAL

No two people will answer Jesus's question the same way because no two callings are the same. Your vision is not supposed to match someone else's. It's not supposed to impress anyone. It's supposed to *move* you. To stretch you. To remind you that there's more inside you than what the world has seen so far.

When Jesus asked that question, He wasn't handing out generic miracles. He was drawing out a personal encounter—and He still is.

So if your vision feels cloudy today, if the future feels clouded—go back to this question.

Sit with it. Pray through it. Ask the Holy Spirit to guide your answer.

"What do you want me to do for you?"

Your answer might just become the blueprint for the next chapter of your life.

STEP FORWARD, SPEAK THE VISION

So let me challenge you: What's your vision? What's the picture in your heart that's so big it scares you and excites you? If you haven't put words to it, start there. Write it out. Refine it. And then, share it. Speak it out loud. It might feel risky. It might feel too bold. But remember—the people in your life aren't waiting for perfection. They're waiting for direction. The world doesn't need more passive leaders. It needs visionaries who are bold enough to see what could be and courageous enough to rally others to build it.

Don't wait for all the answers. Don't let fear silence your calling. Step forward. Speak with conviction. And lead with vision.

Key Highlights

- Vision is the cornerstone of leadership. It defines direction, inspires purpose, and transforms a group into a mission-driven movement.
- Vision must be shared to create alignment. When leaders speak their vision out loud, it clarifies the goal, energizes the team, and creates unity of purpose.
- Bold vision attracts high-level alignment and results.
- Big, daring vision stretches leaders and teams, inspiring excellence, innovation, and long-term impact.
- Vision begins with a personal and honest question. Jesus' question, "What do you want me to do for you?" challenges us to name our desires—because clarity fuels calling.

Reflection Questions

1. What is the current vision that drives your life, leadership, or organization? Can you articulate it clearly in one sentence?
2. Are your daily decisions aligned with your long-term vision? What decisions might you need to revisit through the lens of vision?
3. What part of your vision have you been afraid to say out loud? What keeps you from fully owning and speaking it?

CHAPTER 3

CORE VALUES THAT LEAD THE WAY

When values are clear, decisions are easy.

—ROY E. DISNEY

In the early days of Patagonia, Yvon Chouinard wasn't trying to build a billion-dollar company. He just wanted to make better climbing gear. A blacksmith by trade and a climber by passion, he hand-forged pitons in his backyard and sold them from the back of his car. But even before the world knew the Patagonia name, Chouinard had a core conviction: Business should never come at the cost of the planet.

As Patagonia grew from a humble gear shop into a global outdoor apparel brand, it never lost sight of the values that shaped it. In fact, those values became its compass. From using recycled materials in their clothing to pioneering environmental initiatives long before it was trendy, Patagonia embedded its core values into every decision. One of their guiding principles, "Cause no unnecessary harm," wasn't just a slogan; it was a line in the sand.

When faced with growth opportunities that conflicted with their beliefs, they often walked away. In 2011, Patagonia famously ran a full-page Black Friday ad that read, "Don't Buy This Jacket." It was a bold, countercultural message designed to encourage conscious consumption. Most companies would never dare discourage a sale. But Patagonia wasn't chasing profit. They were pursuing a purpose.

That clarity—anchored in unwavering core values—created not just loyal customers but also a global movement. People didn't just buy Patagonia gear. They bought into what the company stood for.

In 2022, Chouinard made headlines again when he transferred ownership of Patagonia—valued at $3 billion—not to his family, but to a trust and nonprofit that would ensure all profits (roughly $100 million annually) go toward protecting the planet. It was the ultimate expression of alignment between leadership and values.

Yvon Chouinard once said, "I never wanted to be a businessman. I started out of my truck and kept at it for almost 50 years. It's been a half-century of wildness, hard work, and purpose. Hopefully, it will continue like that."

This is what it looks like when core values aren't just posters on a wall—they are the way. They guide decisions, shape culture, attract talent, and inspire impact far beyond the bottom line.

YOUR CORE VALUES ARE YOUR COMPASS

Core values are not just nice-sounding words written on a wall or website. They're your *true north*. They guide your decisions when the path isn't clear. They help you say *yes* to what aligns—and *no* to what doesn't.

For leaders, this compass is everything.

But before you can lead others with conviction, you must do the work of discovering your *own* core values. That takes time. It takes reflection. And it takes courage. Courage to name what truly matters to you and then live it—consistently.

Who are you when no one is watching? What principles do you refuse to compromise on, no matter the cost? What fires you up? What do you deeply believe the world needs more of?

The answers to those questions aren't just for your journal. They're the foundation of how you lead, how you build, and how you influence the culture around you.

SHARED VALUES SHAPE CULTURE

When you're leading a team, your personal values alone aren't enough. You need a *shared* set of core values—ones that your team members believe in and embody. These values must be more than words in an onboarding manual. They must be *lived out loud.*

No one understood this better than S. Truett Cathy, the founder of Chick-fil-A.

Whereas many fast-food giants compete for attention with limited-time offers and aggressive expansion, Chick-fil-A has taken a slower, more intentional path. That path was paved by its founder, S. Truett Cathy—a man of deep faith, conviction, and clarity about what mattered most.

From the beginning, Cathy made decisions rooted in his core values, not in market trends. One of the most iconic—and controversial—was his choice to close all Chick-fil-A locations on Sundays. In an industry where weekends are peak revenue days, this move was almost unthinkable. But for Cathy, it was simple: Sunday was a day for rest, worship, and family. That value was non-negotiable.

What started as a small diner in Hapeville, Georgia, eventually grew into one of the most profitable fast-food chains in the country. And they did it without compromising the very principles that made them different. Cathy once said, "We don't claim to be a Christian business. But we are operated on Christian principles."

Integrity. Excellence. Stewardship. Generosity. These weren't buzzwords in a corporate manual—they were embodied in how the company treated employees, customers, and the communities it served. Chick-fil-A has long invested in leadership development and scholarships for team members, and it quietly contributes millions to charitable causes each year. We will dive further into this in Chapter 5 when we discuss identity.

During the 2013 snowstorm in Atlanta, several motorists were stranded near a local Chick-fil-A. Instead of closing the doors and protecting inventory, the franchise owner opened the restaurant and gave out free food to those in need. When asked why, he simply said, "This is what Truett would've done."

That's the power of core values—they scale far beyond a founder's presence. They create a culture that thinks beyond profits and prioritizes purpose. Even today, Chick-fil-A remains one of the most beloved—and most profitable—restaurant chains in America, despite being open only six days a week.

In Cathy's words: "The true success of a business is not measured by sales or profit, but by the lives it touches and the values it stands for."

When a leader builds on a foundation of values, their legacy outlives them. And in a world driven by short-term gains, organizations like Chick-fil-A remind us that long-term impact is built on values that never waver.

REINFORCE WHAT YOU WANT REPEATED

One of the most powerful tools a leader has is *recognition*. Not the generic "good job" kind, but the specific, values-driven kind that shines a light on behavior you want to see repeated across your entire organization.

When someone on your team lives out a core value, *name it*. Celebrate it. Highlight exactly what they did and why it matters—not to simply spotlight the individual, but to reinforce the *standard*. People need to know what "right" looks like in action. Culture isn't shaped by slogans. It's shaped by stories.

Recently, one of our employees received multiple glowing reviews from residents at one of the communities she manages. These weren't just positive comments—they were heartfelt messages from real people who felt seen, cared for, and well served because of how she showed up every day. She was living out our core values with excellence, empathy, and consistency.

Her direct supervisor didn't keep that to herself. She sent out an email to our entire company—not just to say she was doing well, but to *tell the story* of *why* she was making such an impact. She shared quotes from residents, highlighted her attitude and leadership, and connected it all back to our values. It wasn't about hype. It was about alignment.

And soon, I'll be making a personal visit to that community—not with a formal award or a trophy, but with a sincere "thank you." I want to look her in the eyes and let her know just how much we appreciate her. That kind of personal recognition—the kind that says, "We see you, and you matter"—can fill someone's tank for months.

But here's the ripple effect: When others on the team see that kind of behavior being noticed and celebrated, it elevates the entire culture. It signals to everyone, *This is who we are. This is what we value. This is what we pursue together.*

Every act of recognition is a *seed*. Every story shared about someone modeling the mission is *water* for the culture you're cultivating.

If you want your team to internalize what matters most, don't just tell them—*show them*. Live it. Highlight it. Repeat it. Reinforce it in emails, meetings, and one-on-one moments.

Culture doesn't grow by accident. It grows through intentional praise, courageous correction, and clear reinforcement of the values that define who you are and where you're going.

And remember this: What gets rewarded gets repeated.

NO COMPROMISE

One of the most difficult responsibilities of leadership is protecting the integrity of your culture—especially when it means making hard decisions about people. No matter how talented or productive a team member may be, if they consistently violate your core values, they will do more harm than good.

The truth is, values misalignment is contagious. It only takes one person operating outside the boundaries of your culture to cause others to question whether your values are real or just words on a wall. When you allow behavior that contradicts what you claim to stand for, it sends a message that performance is more important than principles. That kind of compromise doesn't just weaken morale—it erodes trust.

As a leader, you must be willing to draw the line and say, "We don't do that here." Not out of harshness or judgment, but because you are building something worth protecting.

Core values are the guardrails that keep your organization on mission. Great leaders don't just talk about those values—they live them, defend them, and, when necessary, make the tough calls to ensure their team remains aligned and healthy.

Back in 2012, the Golden State Warriors made a controversial decision that left many fans scratching their heads. At the time, Monta Ellis was the team's star player—explosive, exciting, and the leading scorer. He was beloved by the fanbase and put up big numbers every night. But behind the scenes, it was clear to the organization's leadership that Monta wasn't a long-term fit for the culture they were trying to build. He was talented, no doubt, but the style of play and mindset he brought to the locker room didn't align with the unselfish, team-first values that would later define the Warriors dynasty.

So they made a bold move: They traded Monta Ellis.

In return, they doubled down on a relatively unproven, quieter leader—a young Steph Curry, who up to that point had been battling ankle injuries and hadn't yet become a household name. But Curry embodied the values the Warriors wanted to build around: humility, work ethic, team-oriented play, and belief in something bigger than personal stats.

The reaction to the trade was immediate—and negative. Fans booed the team's owner during a public appearance. Many thought the Warriors had made a huge mistake.

But the organization stayed the course.

Within a few seasons, Golden State had built a culture where values and chemistry mattered as much as raw talent. And in 2015, just three years after letting go of their leading scorer, the Warriors won their first NBA Championship in 40 years. Not by chasing stars—but by aligning their roster with their core values.

Letting go of a top performer is never easy—especially when they're the face of your team. But value violations, even subtle ones, can keep you from becoming who you're meant to be. Sometimes the road to greatness begins with the courage to say, "We're building something bigger than one person."

LET VALUES LEAD

Core values are more than words—they are the invisible force steering everything you build. They determine who joins your team and who leaves it. They shape the experience of your customers, the morale of your employees, and the legacy of your leadership.

If you want to build something that lasts, something that carries meaning beyond the next quarter or the next project, then you must let your values lead. That starts with doing the deep work of defining them for yourself. Then, it means inviting your team into that same clarity, rallying around shared convictions that are more than decorative—they're *definitive*.

It's easy to compromise in the name of growth. Easy to overlook small violations in the name of performance. But leadership isn't about doing what's easy. It's about doing what's right—especially when it costs you.

The organizations that endure—from Patagonia to Chick-fil-A to championship teams—are the ones whose leaders have the courage to say, *"This is who we are, and this is how we operate."*

So choose your values. Preach them often. Reinforce them through recognition. Protect them with discipline.

Because in the end, culture doesn't rise to the level of your vision—it rests on the strength of your values.

Let them lead the way.

Key Highlights

- Core values are a leader's compass. They guide decisions, clarify direction, and ensure alignment—especially in uncertain or high-pressure moments.
- Strong values create lasting culture.
- Publicly celebrating team members who embody your values sets a standard and encourages those behaviors to be repeated across the organization.
- Don't compromise on values—even with top performers. Allowing value misalignment for the sake of talent damages trust and culture; real leadership makes the tough calls to protect what matters most.
- Values define legacy more than vision alone. Although vision casts direction, it's values that determine how an organization operates, grows, and sustains impact over the long haul.

Reflection Questions

1. When was the last time you made a difficult decision based solely on your values? What was the cost? What was the reward?
2. Where in your life or leadership have you compromised your values for the sake of convenience, profit, or peacekeeping? What lesson did you take from that moment?
3. How visible are your values in your organization, team, or home?

PART TWO
THE INNER WORK OF LEADERSHIP

CHAPTER 4

LEADING YOURSELF FIRST

The first and best victory is to conquer self.

—PLATO

In the darkest corners of humanity, Viktor Frankl discovered a truth that would guide millions.

Frankl, a neurologist and psychiatrist, survived the horrors of Nazi concentration camps during World War II. He lost his parents, his brother, and his pregnant wife. Everything was stripped from him—his family, his career, his dignity, his freedom. In those camps, where hope was scarce and cruelty was the norm, many gave in to despair. But Frankl held on to one thing that could not be taken from him: the power to choose his response.

He watched as men around him lost their will to live, crushed by suffering, starvation, and sorrow. But he also witnessed something miraculous: that even in the most inhumane conditions imaginable, some men rose above their circumstances. They encouraged others, shared their last piece of bread, prayed quietly, and carried themselves with purpose.

Frankl realized that true leadership begins with how you carry yourself in crisis. It's not about power. It's about presence. It's not about control. It's about character. He chose to lead himself with dignity, with discipline, and with hope, and in doing so, he gave others permission to do the same.

In his bestselling book, *Man's Search for Meaning*, Frankl wrote, "Everything can be taken from a man but one thing: the last of the human freedoms, which is to choose one's attitude in any given set of circumstances."

The decision to lead yourself first, even when life is completely out of your control, is what made Frankl a true leader. He didn't have a title. He had no followers in the traditional sense. But he led himself with clarity, purpose, and hope. And because of that, he became a beacon of light to those around him.

In a very different setting, one without prison walls or barbed wire, Jesus demonstrated this same principle of leading yourself before leading others. Before beginning His public ministry, before calling a single disciple, before preaching to the crowds or healing the sick, Jesus withdrew into the wilderness for 40 days. There, He faced hunger, isolation, and the relentless temptation of Satan. There was no audience, no applause, no visible "impact." It was just Him, His Father, and the battle within.

In that solitude, Jesus showed that true leadership begins in the private places where no one is watching. He mastered Himself through God's guidance and anchored His heart to God's Word, refusing to be swayed by comfort, compromise, or the shortcut to power. If He had failed in the wilderness, He could never have succeeded in His mission. But because He led Himself first, He was able to lead others with authority, integrity, and unwavering purpose.

Just as Frankl chose his attitude in the darkest of circumstances, Jesus chose faithfulness in the face of temptation. And that victory in private became the foundation for His victory in public.

Before you can lead anyone else, you have to learn how to lead yourself. It makes sense, doesn't it? Yet somehow, it's the most overlooked principle in leadership. We spend so much time looking outward—fixing others, critiquing what needs to change around us—and far too little time looking inward.

Why? Because it's easier. It's easier to tell someone else how to improve than it is to confront your own inconsistencies. It's easier to scroll, distract, and blame than it is to reflect, discipline, and grow. But leadership doesn't begin with commanding others. It begins with mastering yourself.

Here are the five foundational areas I've found to be essential in leading yourself effectively:

1. **Build a winning mindset**
2. **Get in touch with your spirit**
3. **Protect and nurture your energy**
4. **Be intentional with your time**
5. **Curate your environment**

BUILD A WINNING MINDSET

Your mind is your most powerful asset. It can create momentum or sabotage it. It can be a breeding ground for doubt and distraction or a launchpad for focus, confidence, and action.

The human mind is relentless. It replays the past, fears the future, resists the present. It overthinks, catastrophizes, and lies to us on a regular basis. But here's the beauty of the mind: It can be trained.

Just like a muscle, your mindset gets stronger with consistent, intentional effort. If you want to lead others well, you must first learn to lead your thoughts.

How? Feed your mind better input.

For me, reading has been the most powerful tool in reshaping how I think. I've read over 400 books in the past eight years. Not to impress anyone, but to grow. Some of those books were helpful. A few were transformational. Titles like *Think and Grow Rich* by Napoleon Hill, *Mindset* by Carol Dweck, *Psycho-Cybernetics* by Maxwell Maltz, and *How to Win Friends and Influence People* by Dale

Carnegie didn't just fill my head with ideas—they rewired the way I see the world and myself.

Watch your thoughts, for they become words.
Watch your words, for they become actions.
Watch your actions, for they become habits.
Watch your habits, for they become character.
Watch your character, for it becomes your destiny.

—UNKNOWN

This isn't just about positive thinking. It's about intentional, disciplined thinking. It's about choosing what you allow into your mental space. It's about noticing the narrative in your head and learning how to redirect it.

Because what you think determines how you lead.

When your mind is governed by fear, pride, or ego, your leadership will reflect it. But when your mind is aligned with truth, wisdom, and the Spirit of God, your leadership becomes a source of peace, strength, and vision for others.

So start building your mindset like you would your body: with consistency, challenge, and quality fuel. Read daily. Reflect often. Be ruthless about what you allow to shape your thoughts. Because the battle for leadership starts in the mind.

GET IN TOUCH WITH YOUR SPIRIT

Incorporating Scripture and quiet time with God has radically shifted my leadership and my life. When you begin to recognize that we are spiritual beings navigating a temporary, earthly journey, everything starts to shift. Your perspective expands. Your problems shrink. Your priorities realign.

The most influential and grounded leaders I've studied or personally known all draw from something deeper than intellect or charisma. They lead from their soul.

When I'm spiritually grounded, I make decisions with greater clarity. I trust my instincts. I feel a boldness that comes not from ego but from alignment with something higher. I believe God wired us to be attuned to His voice, and when we slow down enough to listen, that spiritual intuition, that "sixth sense," becomes clearer.

A verse that's shaped how I view spiritual alignment is:

> *But seek first [God's] kingdom and his*
> *righteousness, and all these things will be given to*
> *you as well.*
>
> —MATTHEW 6:33 (NIV)

That's not just a verse about provision, it's a principle for leadership. When you prioritize your spiritual health, everything else in your life begins to fall into place.

In a world full of noise and distraction, leading yourself spiritually may be the most radical and necessary leadership practice of all.

PROTECT AND NURTURE YOUR ENERGY AT ALL COSTS

Energy is your leadership fuel. Without it, your decisions, your focus, your creativity, and your compassion all come to a grinding halt. You can have the best intentions, the clearest goals, and the most exciting vision, but if your energy is depleted, your execution will fall short.

Have you ever tried leading when you're sick, burned out, or sleep-deprived? It's almost impossible to show up fully. Even a minor dip in your energy can cloud your thinking, shorten your patience, and make every task feel heavier.

Now flip that. Think about the days when your energy is high—when you're rested, fueled, and present. You move differently. You speak with conviction. You make clearer decisions. You create momentum without forcing it. You're in rhythm.

Leadership requires more than vision. It requires **vitality**.

And that means protecting your energy is *strategic*. It's a form of stewardship. Because when your tank is empty, you can't lead anyone well.

Once I got serious about living a healthier lifestyle, I began to see a ripple effect in every other area of my life. I had more capacity for the people I loved. I had more focus in my work. I felt stronger, more confident, and more grounded.

One of the biggest game changers for me has been my morning routine. Truthfully, I'm not perfect at it (I'd say I hit it about 75 percent of the time) but when I do, my energy and productivity go through the roof. If I had to boil my success down to one consistent practice, it would be this.

Here's what my "perfect morning" looks like:

- **4:30 a.m.:** Wake up and make coffee
- **4:35 a.m.:** Open the Bible and spend time in the Word
- **4:50 a.m.:** Journal
- **5:00 a.m.:** Read (or in the past six-plus months, write) something motivational
- **6:00 a.m.:** Exercise
- **7:00 a.m.:** Get ready for the day
- **7:30 a.m.:** Out the door to the office

The compound effect of stacking these daily habits over time is hard to explain. Not only does it give me a sense of accomplishment first thing in the morning, but it also fuels my confidence for the rest of the day. Discipline is what makes it work at first, but eventually it just becomes who you are.

And yes, this only works because I go to bed early. Most nights I'm in bed around 8:00 p.m. I've tried running on six hours of sleep, and it doesn't cut it for me. I need eight hours if I'm going to show up at my best.

This rhythm multiplies my energy. It's a form of stewardship over the one resource every leader must guard: their vitality.

I still have days off, and I'm certainly not perfect with my routines. But I've learned that being intentional about energy is essential. And the best leaders I know don't just *manage* their energy; they fiercely protect it.

Your body isn't a machine to be pushed until it breaks. It's a temple to be honored. So fuel it with food that sustains you. Move it daily, even when it's inconvenient. Rest deeply. Set boundaries around the things that drain you. Create space for stillness and recovery. Guard your mornings. Build rhythms that restore you.

Your energy is a non-negotiable asset. Protect it at all costs.

BE INTENTIONAL WITH YOUR TIME

Time is the great equalizer. We all get 24 hours. So why do some people seem to accomplish ten times more?

That question used to frustrate me. But after reading countless biographies and listening to hundreds of episodes of my favorite podcast—*Founders* by David Senra—I noticed a clear pattern:

The most effective leaders in history are ruthless with their time.

They don't just have routines. They have rhythms: intentional patterns for their days, their mornings, their deep work, and their rest. They treat time like a non-renewable resource because that's exactly what it is.

Great leaders don't tolerate wasting time; they own every minute. They schedule the important before the urgent. They say no to good things so they can say yes to great things. They block out time to think, to reflect, to be still. They know that clarity comes when you create space and not stay deep in the weeds at all times.

One of the best frameworks I've ever learned for managing time with intention comes from Dan Sullivan's Strategic Coach program. He breaks time down into three categories: Focus Days, Buffer Days, and Free Days.

- **Focus Days** are for your highest-value activities: the things only you can do that create the most growth, revenue, or impact. For a leader, that might mean vision casting, meeting with key partners, closing deals, or creating new opportunities. On these days, distractions are minimized and energy is maximized.
- **Buffer Days** are the preparation days. They're where you handle the admin, the planning, the clean-up, the learning, and the behind-the-scenes work that makes your Focus Days more effective. Done right, Buffer Days create margin so you can step into Focus Days fully ready.
- **Free Days** are exactly what they sound like, 24-hour periods with no work. Not checking emails, not sneaking in calls, not "just one quick task." Free Days are for rest, renewal, fun, family, faith, and health. They allow you to recharge so that your Focus Days are sharper and more productive.

This framework forces you to be intentional instead of reactive. It pushes you to prioritize your *unique ability* (as coined by Dan Sullivan, Strategic Coach) and gives you the space to actually live, not just work. And as counterintuitive as it may feel, the more ruthlessly you protect Free Days and design Buffer Days, the more effective and profitable your Focus Days become.

The truth is, you can't become who you were created to be if you're constantly at the mercy of distraction. Social media, texts, endless scrolling, news, and opinions will never help you build the future you want. The only way to rise above is to build habits and structures around the life you say you want.

Teach us to number our days,
that we may gain a heart of wisdom.

—Psalm 90:12 (NIV)

Wisdom begins when we recognize the limited time we've been given and use it with purpose.

CURATE YOUR ENVIRONMENT

Who you surround yourself with is one of the most important leadership decisions you'll ever make.

Your environment is always speaking to you. Every conversation, every room, every text thread is shaping your mindset and fueling your habits, whether you realize it or not. Leadership isn't just about who *follows* you. It's also about who *walks with* you.

Negativity, laziness, gossip, and small thinking are all very contagious. If you spend your time around people who make excuses and play small, you'll start to mirror that behavior without even realizing it.

But the inverse is also true. Get around people who dream big, speak life, and stretch themselves, and you'll find yourself rising too. You become like the people you spend the most time with. So choose wisely.

The hard part? Changing your environment often requires courage. It might mean redefining relationships, saying no to old routines, or stepping away from people you've known for years. It might mean walking alone for a season before you find your tribe. But if you want more for your life, you'll have to make tough choices.

I've taken this principle seriously in my own life. Over the years, I've made a conscious effort to invest heavily in the environments I place myself in. Sometimes that has meant "paying to play." I've invested a significant amount of money joining different mastermind communities filled with like-minded individuals who push me in ways I could never have imagined. I've been part of Strategic Coach, Raisemasters, Vistage, and most recently, I joined a group called ELEVATED.

Each of these rooms has stretched me in unique ways, forcing me to think bigger, raise my standards, and sharpen my leadership. But I've also experienced the power of free communities. One of the most valuable groups I'm in is the men's small group at my church. The conversations, accountability, and brotherhood in that room have been just as impactful on my growth as the high-dollar masterminds.

I personally believe this is a cheat code in life. By choosing the right rooms, you make the world smaller and elevate your inner circle. And when your inner circle rises, so do you.

> *Walk with the wise and become wise, for a*
> *companion of fools suffers harm.*
>
> —PROVERBS 13:20 (NIV)

Discomfort is often the doorway to growth. And sometimes, the most strategic move you can make as a leader is changing the room you're in.

A PERSONAL SHIFT

My journey toward self-leadership didn't begin with a perfectly timed motivational quote or a goal-setting seminar. It began in one of the hardest seasons of my life, after my dad passed away.

Losing him shook something deep in me. It forced me to confront the reality that life is short, fragile, and unpredictable. It made me look at how I was spending my time, how I was showing up in the world, and who I was becoming. There's something about death that makes you reflect with uncomfortable honesty. For me, it was a wake-up call. I started asking deeper questions. I began to take personal growth more seriously, not just for success, but for legacy. I didn't want to waste my life, and I didn't want to dishonor the values my dad had instilled in me.

That season marked the beginning of a shift in my mindset and my habits. I started to realize that leadership wasn't about image; it was about integrity. About doing the hard, internal work of becoming the kind of man others could trust and follow.

I've always had a strong desire to succeed. But for years, my actions didn't align with my ambition. I said I wanted to lead, to build, to make a positive difference in people's lives, but my habits told a different story.

However, transformation doesn't happen overnight. While my dad passing sparked some positive changes, I was still falling into poor decision making from time to time.

The real change began when I met Peyton, my now wife. Her faith, strength, and vision challenged me in the best possible ways. She helped me realize that true success is about the quiet, consistent, sometimes unglamorous choices you make every single day.

There's a quote I love, which has been attributed to several people, including John Demelo, Rob Hill, and Alex Okoroji:

> *A man with dreams needs a woman with vision.*
> *Her perspective, faith, and support will change his*
> *reality.*

That's been my story. Peyton saw in me what I hadn't yet fully owned in myself. And because of her influence, I started making different decisions—better decisions. I had a decent foundation, but I got more serious about my mornings, my health, my prayer life, and my goals.

And here's the truth I learned:

Your life is made up of a collection of your daily actions.

The good news? You can make a new choice *today.* You can start building new habits *today.* You can begin leading yourself better *right now.*

Because if you want to lead others with clarity and strength, you must first lead the person staring back at you in the mirror.

This is where leadership begins. Before you can build teams, lead organizations, or inspire others, you must first learn to lead the one person you'll be with for the rest of your life: yourself.

Every great leader I know started with this step. They looked in the mirror. They told the truth. They started doing the hard, often invisible work that few applaud but everyone feels.

Your mindset. Your spirit. Your health. Your time. Your environment.

Get those in alignment, and you'll lay a foundation strong enough to carry whatever future God entrusts to you.

So let's get clear: you don't have to be perfect to lead. But you do have to be responsible. You have to take ownership of your choices, your patterns, and your path.

Because once you learn to lead yourself with excellence, you'll be ready to lead others with impact.

Key Highlights

- Self-leadership is the foundation of all leadership. True leadership begins not with influence over others, but with discipline, character, and integrity in your own life—especially when no one is watching.
- Your thoughts drive your behavior, habits, and destiny. Training your mind through intentional input (books, reflection, truth) is essential to leading yourself well.
- Energy and time must be protected with discipline. Stewarding your physical vitality and being intentional with your time (through routines, rhythms, and boundaries) directly impacts your ability to lead effectively.
- Your environment determines your elevation. The people and spaces you surround yourself with shape your growth and mindset. Great leaders intentionally curate their circles to reflect the values and vision they pursue.

Reflection Questions

1. In what area of your life do you need to start leading yourself more intentionally the most—your mindset, spirit, body, time, or environment? Why?
2. What's one daily habit you can commit to this week that will move you closer to the leader you want to become?
3. What limiting thought or story are you believing that's holding you back from fully owning your leadership potential?

CHAPTER 5

Identity Before
Influence

It is not what we do that determines who we are.
It is who we are that determines what we do.

—Charles F. Stanley

In his bestselling book, *Atomic Habits*, James Clear makes a powerful distinction between outcomes, processes, and identity. Most people, he says, focus on outcomes: losing weight, making more money, leading a team. Some go deeper and build systems to support their goals. But the most lasting change starts at the deepest level: identity.

Clear writes that true behavior change is identity change. You don't just say, "I want to run a marathon." You say, "I'm a runner." You don't just want to read more books. You begin to see yourself as a reader. That shift changes everything.

The same principle applies to leadership.

Before Truett Cathy ever built Chick-fil-A into a national brand, he built something far more important: a foundation of character.

Cathy grew up during the Great Depression, helping support his family from a young age. Life was hard, but instead of becoming bitter or being driven by ambition alone, he developed a deep-rooted belief in integrity, generosity, and faith.

When he opened his first restaurant, the Dwarf Grill (later renamed the Dwarf House), he wasn't focused on building an empire. He was focused on serving people well—honestly, humbly, and with excellence. His identity as a follower of Christ shaped everything he did, from how he treated employees to the decision to close on Sundays, even when competitors stayed open and profits could have soared.

Cathy often said, "It's better to build boys than mend men," reflecting his lifelong commitment to mentoring young people and investing in their character before worrying about their output.

Even as Chick-fil-A expanded, he refused to compromise on the values that had shaped him early in life. He knew who he was, and because of that, he didn't chase trends, bow to cultural pressure, or sacrifice principles for growth.

Truett Cathy's leadership wasn't about performing for the crowd. It was about being rooted in purpose. His life and leadership flowed from identity, and that made all the difference.

Another example of identity shaping influence is Sam Walton, the founder of Wal-Mart.

Walton didn't start with a dream of building the largest retailer in the world. He started with a simple commitment to serving customers better than anyone else.

Raised during the Great Depression, Walton learned the values of hard work, frugality, and honesty early in life. Long before Wal-Mart became a national phenomenon, he was known for his relentless work ethic and his humility. He drove an old pickup truck, wore inexpensive clothes, and spent time walking store aisles, talking directly to employees and customers.

Walton's leadership wasn't fueled by a need for fame or wealth. It was fueled by a clear identity: He saw himself first and foremost as a servant. Someone who created opportunity, listened carefully, and never thought he was above anyone else.

His consistency in small things—like treating every associate with dignity or obsessing over ways to save customers a few cents—eventually built a retail empire. But the foundation wasn't flash or ambition. It was humility, consistency, and character, lived out daily, long before the world ever noticed.

Before you can influence others with authenticity and consistency, you must know who you are. You must build your leadership on the foundation of identity—not image, not approval, not ambition. Because if your identity is rooted in anything temporary, your influence will be too.

If you don't know who you are, the world will try to tell you who to be. And if you chase influence without identity, you'll burn out—or worse, build success that's hollow.

True influence begins when you lead from the inside out.

KNOW WHO YOU ARE BEFORE YOU TELL OTHERS WHAT TO DO

Another great example of a leader who helped change the course of history and embodied this trait was the 16th President of the United States. Before Abraham Lincoln ever became known as one of history's greatest leaders, he was deeply acquainted with defeat.

Lincoln lost multiple elections, suffered business failures, and endured profound personal tragedies. Yet despite the setbacks, he remained remarkably steady because he had an unwavering internal compass.

During the Civil War, when the nation was literally tearing itself apart, Lincoln didn't chase popularity or public favor. He wasn't trying to be liked. He was anchored in a deeper sense of calling and conviction about who he was and what he was meant to do. His leadership flowed from a place of identity, not insecurity.

In one of his personal letters, he wrote, "I am not bound to win, but I am bound to be true."

That is the essence of leading from identity. Lincoln's legacy wasn't built on charisma. It wasn't built on public image. It was built on character. Before he ever told a divided country what they needed to do, he knew who he was, and that made all the difference.

We live in a world that celebrates influence, platform, and visibility, but often overlooks identity. Social media rewards performance. Business culture celebrates achievement. But leadership without a strong identity is like a skyscraper built on sand. It might rise quickly, but it won't last.

The strongest leaders I've met aren't driven by external validation. They're rooted in something deeper. They know who they are.

And knowing who you are isn't just about having a personality profile or listing your strengths and weaknesses. It's about getting honest with yourself. It's about asking the hard questions:

- What do I believe about myself when no one's watching?
- Where do I find my worth?
- Am I leading from a place of security or from a need to prove something?
- What values am I actually living out?

Most people live out a version of themselves that's been shaped by culture, family expectations, past wounds, or their own inner critic. They adapt to survive, to be liked, to avoid failure. But over time, that survival identity becomes their default setting. And that's dangerous because you can't lead others well when you're still hiding from yourself.

You have to excavate before you build.

If you want to lead from a place of purpose and peace, you must dig beneath the surface. You must unlearn the lies you've believed about yourself. You must stop outsourcing your identity to other people's opinions. And you must choose to return to who God says you are.

For we are God's handiwork, created in Christ
Jesus to do good works, which God prepared in
advance for us to do.

—EPHESIANS 2:10 (NIV)

That's not just motivational. That's identity. You were created with intention. On purpose. For a purpose.

Before you lead anyone else, slow down long enough to lead yourself back to the truth about who you are. Because the strength of your influence will never exceed the clarity of your identity.

THE POWER OF SELF-AWARENESS

Fred Rogers, known simply as "Mister Rogers" to millions, was one of the most quietly influential leaders of the twentieth century.

Unlike most public figures, Rogers didn't lead with charisma or force of personality. He led with gentleness, authenticity, and profound emotional intelligence.

Before he ever spoke into a microphone or stood before a camera, Rogers spent years studying theology, child psychology, and communication. He understood the weight of words, the power of presence, and the responsibility of influence. He knew that every interaction, every tone of voice, every facial expression could either build someone up or tear them down.

Rogers was intensely aware of his own emotions. He once said, "Anything that's human is mentionable, and anything that is mentionable can be more manageable." He practiced acknowledging his feelings rather than pretending they didn't exist. And because he managed himself well, he was able to model emotional regulation for millions of children and parents alike.

Behind the scenes, Rogers famously took great care before public appearances, preparing not just his notes but his *spirit*. He would often pray, reflect, and ask himself how he wanted others to feel after being with him.

His leadership wasn't about controlling people. It was about stewarding presence.

Mister Rogers showed that self-awareness is one of the greatest strengths a leader can have. Because when you understand yourself, you're far better equipped to understand and care for others.

Self-awareness is the bridge between who you are and how you lead. It's the ability to observe your thoughts, habits, tendencies, and triggers with honesty and humility. Without it, you can have the best intentions but still cause confusion, misalignment, or even harm.

I've seen incredibly talented leaders stall out or self-sabotage because they lacked awareness. They didn't see how they were coming across. They didn't understand how their tone impacted others. They weren't aware of how their stress bled into the team. And maybe worst of all, they weren't open to feedback.

Self-awareness allows you to grow. It opens the door to feedback. It gives you insight into how others experience you and how to adjust in ways that build trust and influence. It's not about perfection. It's about ownership.

Ask yourself:

- Which patterns in my leadership are helping me, and which ones are holding me back?
- How do people experience me when I'm under pressure?
- Where do I tend to react rather than respond?
- What feedback have I received consistently—but resisted?

You must know yourself to grow yourself.

—JOHN MAXWELL

That's not just a quote; it's a roadmap. Self-awareness isn't something you stumble into. It's something you seek on purpose. When you begin to see your patterns, your blind spots, and your tendencies, you gain the ability to make meaningful, lasting change.

When you cultivate self-awareness, you gain the power to lead with empathy and emotional intelligence. And that's what sets great leaders apart—they don't just move people; they understand them. And that understanding starts with understanding yourself.

IDENTITY IS BUILT ON CHARACTER, INTEGRITY, AND CONSISTENCY

For a faith-centered leader, identity is received before it is achieved. Before Jesus ever preached a sermon or called a disciple, the Father named Him: "This is my beloved Son" (Matthew 3:17 ESV). Only then came the wilderness where that identity was tested (Matthew 4). That's the pattern: identity affirmed, then character forged, then influence entrusted. Lasting leadership still follows that order.

Before John Wooden ever became a legendary basketball coach, he was a teacher of character.

Wooden didn't win ten NCAA national championships by focusing only on skills or strategy. He built his teams on a foundation of integrity, discipline, and consistency.

One of his most famous lessons was the simple, repeated act of teaching every new player how to properly put on their socks and tie their shoes. It sounds trivial, almost laughable. But Wooden knew that small neglects lead to bigger failures. A wrinkle in a sock could cause a blister. A loose shoe could cause a stumble.

Wooden believed that excellence was built in the quiet, unseen habits of preparation and discipline. He lived it himself, showing up early, planning meticulously, modeling humility.

His players knew: the man they saw under the bright lights was the same man they saw in private. Calm. Steady. Humble. Demanding excellence, but never by yelling or manipulating. Always by modeling.

Wooden once said, "Be more concerned with your character than your reputation, because your character is what you really are, while your reputation is merely what others think you are." Scripture says it this way: "People look at the outward appearance, but the LORD looks at the heart" (1 Samuel 16:7 NIV).

His leadership wasn't built in championships. It was built in consistency. And because his identity was rooted in character, not performance, his influence outlived his career and continues to shape leaders today.

At the core of every strong identity is something deeper than talent or personality: it's character. Character is who you are when no one's watching. It's what you return to under pressure. It's the internal compass that guides your decisions when the spotlight is off.

And that character is only as strong as your integrity. When your private life matches your public leadership, you earn trust. Not just the trust of others, but the trust in yourself.

Consistency is what gives integrity its power. Anyone can have a good day. Anyone can post a powerful message or lead a meeting with confidence. But real leadership is built in the quiet repetition of daily discipline. Showing up. Following through. Doing the right thing, even when it costs you something. Over time, those repetitions look like the fruit of the Spirit—"love, joy, peace, forbearance, kindness, goodness, faithfulness, gentleness and self-control"— growing steady and visible (Galatians 5:22–23 NIV).

People don't follow charisma forever. They follow character over time. They follow leaders who are steady, not just inspiring. Who are consistent, not just impressive.

You want to build lasting influence? Don't start with your platform. Start with your private life. Build an identity rooted in integrity and shaped by character, and over time, your influence will take care of itself.

You may have noticed a pattern throughout the stories in this chapter:

Before Truett Cathy built a national brand, he built a foundation of character.

Before Sam Walton led a retail revolution, he lived a life of humility and service.

Before Abraham Lincoln preserved a nation, he developed an unwavering inner compass.

Before John Wooden won championships, he mastered the small disciplines of daily integrity.

Before Mister Rogers became a cultural icon, he cultivated self-awareness and emotional wisdom.

This was not by accident. It was by design. Great leaders establish their identity **before** they are recognized as great leaders and **before** they accomplish great things. They don't wait for success to tell them who they are. They decide who they are. And as mentioned earlier, the believer receives who they are in Christ: "God's handiwork, created in Christ Jesus to do good works" (Ephesians 2:10 NIV). Then success follows as stewardship.

That's the invitation for you and me. Do the necessary work now. Dig deep. Get clear. Build your identity on a foundation of character, integrity, and consistency while the world isn't watching and while the spotlight isn't shining. When the time comes and your opportunity arrives, you won't have to scramble to figure out who you are. You'll already know. And that clarity will be the reason your leadership lasts.

Key Highlights

- True and lasting leadership begins with identity—not just goals, habits, or titles. Who you *are* determines what you *do*, and authentic influence flows from a secure inner foundation.
- Character and integrity are the core of lasting leadership.
- Self-awareness fuels emotional intelligence and influence. Self-awareness allows for empathy, honest feedback, and meaningful growth.
- Leadership must be rooted before it is recognized. Great leaders establish identity and character *before* achieving success.
- For Christian leaders, identity is not self-made but *God-given*. Anchoring leadership in faith creates clarity, purpose, and sustainability that outlasts trends or trials.

Reflection Questions

1. How do I intentionally prepare myself (mentally, emotionally, or spiritually) before engaging with others?
2. When the spotlight is off, do my actions align with my values?
3. What feedback have I consistently resisted? What might that reveal about areas I could improve in?

CHAPTER 6

OVERCOMING
FEAR & FAILURE

*Success is not final, failure is not fatal: It is the
courage to continue that counts.*

—WINSTON CHURCHILL

THE FALL BEFORE THE RISE: A STORY OF
PERSEVERANCE

In 1994, a young entrepreneur named Howard Schultz walked
into the office of his fledgling company, Starbucks, with a heavy
heart. The company was bleeding money. Investors were growing
impatient. His grand vision of transforming a local Seattle coffee
shop into a global third space, somewhere between home and work,
seemed unrealistic at best, laughable at worst. He had been turned
down by over 200 investors. His team was skeptical. His competitors
were scoffing. And still, he pressed on.

Schultz's story is now legend. He didn't walk away. He didn't
scale down the dream. He doubled down on it out of conviction.

He believed in the mission. He believed that creating a place where people could gather, converse, and connect over a cup of coffee could actually transform culture.

That transformation didn't happen overnight. It happened after years of setbacks, product failures, brand confusion, and leadership challenges. Yet Schultz's grit in the face of fear and his refusal to accept failure as final paved the way for Starbucks to become a household name in over 80 countries.

This is not just a business success story. It's a leadership story. It's a story of confronting fear and leveraging failure as fuel. The good news is that Howard Schultz's story isn't all that unique. Go back and research just about any great leader, and you will read about a time when their back was against the wall and they were on the brink of utter failure. The one thing they all have in common? They didn't quit.

THE INVISIBLE CHAINS: LIMITING BELIEFS

"You're not good enough." "This will never work." "You're not ready." "You're going to look foolish." Do these sound familiar? These thoughts are rooted not in truth but in fear. They're the echoes of past disappointments, the voices of critics, the bruises from our own self-doubt. Left unchecked, they form the invisible chains that keep us from stepping into our God-given potential.

Limiting beliefs are dangerous not because they are loud but because they are subtle. They masquerade as wisdom. They present themselves as caution. But they're not wisdom; they're fear in disguise.

And here's the truth: those lies don't come from God. Scripture says in 2 Timothy 1:7 (NKJV), "For God has not given us a spirit of fear, but of power and of love and of a sound mind." Christ-centered leadership means silencing fear's lies with God's truth, and leading from a place of Spirit-given power rather than insecurity.

The greatest freedom I've found is learning to acknowledge those thoughts but refusing to accept them as my own. The fear may come knocking, but it doesn't get to stay. It doesn't decide my next step. It doesn't get to write my story. Only God does.

The Magic of Discomfort

I often tell my team: "Get comfortable being uncomfortable." We've all heard that saying, but how much thought have you actually given it? Think about it. Every breakthrough in your life probably started with some kind of discomfort. The hard conversation. The leap of faith. The risk you weren't sure you were ready to take.

Discomfort isn't a signal to retreat; it's a sign that you're stretching. And it's in the stretching that real strength is built. So, the next time you're in a group setting and feel the urge to speak up or ask a question and your heart starts pounding, don't let fear win. Speak up anyway. Do it once, then again. After three or four times, you'll notice the fear starts to fade, or, at the very least, it won't control you the way it used to.

For me, the moments of greatest discomfort have almost always been the precursors to something meaningful. I remember when I first launched my business. I had no idea what I was doing. I felt like an imposter most days. Fear gripped me. What if I failed? What if I embarrassed myself? What if I let my future family down?

But I didn't let the fear call the shots. I took action. That's been my go-to strategy every time fear tries to paralyze me. I just start doing something. Anything. Because I've found that action quiets fear. And you know what happened? I learned. I got better. I experienced a few wins and slowly started gaining more and more confidence.

Fear thrives in the hypothetical. It spins a thousand "what ifs" and worst-case scenarios. But when you start moving, when you take that first step, the fog begins to lift. You realize it's not nearly as bad as your mind made it out to be. You gain perspective. You gain momentum.

Leaders Feel Fear—They Just Don't Bow to It

There's a myth that great leaders are fearless. That's not true. The truth is, great leaders feel fear; they just don't let it slow them down.

They act in spite of fear. They press forward in spite of doubt. They walk into the storm, knowing that courage isn't the absence of fear; it's obedience in the face of it.

As a leader, you will face fear constantly:

- Fear of failure
- Fear of disappointing others
- Fear of being misunderstood
- Fear of making the wrong decision
- Fear of the unknown

But those fears don't have to dictate your behavior. The more you take action in the face of fear, the more confidence you build—not from success, but from simply *showing up.*

THE GIFT OF FAILURE

Yes, you read that right. Failure is a gift, if you let it be.

Some of my greatest breakthroughs have come on the other side of massive disappointments. Deals that fell through. Hires that didn't work out. Ideas that bombed. Opportunities that vanished.

But here's what I've learned: Failure is only final if you quit. If you keep going, failure becomes a stepping stone.

Scripture reminds us of this truth. James 1:2–4 (NIV) says, "Consider it pure joy, my brothers and sisters, whenever you face trials of many kinds, because you know that the testing of your faith produces perseverance. Let perseverance finish its work so that you may be mature and complete, not lacking anything." In other words, our failures and setbacks are building in us the perseverance we'll need for greater leadership ahead. Failure isn't the enemy. Quitting is.

Thomas Edison once said, "I have not failed. I've just found 10,000 ways that won't work." That kind of mindset separates leaders from spectators.

Leaders *fail forward.*

When you hit a wall, don't change the goal; change the plan. If your path isn't working, don't assume the dream is broken. Get creative. Get resourceful. Ask for help. Learn a new skill. Pivot your approach. But don't shrink the goal just because the path got hard.

Every successful person you admire has a trail of failure behind them. What sets them apart is not the absence of setbacks but their willingness to *fail fast, learn fast, and try again.*

THE REAL GOAL ISN'T PERFECTION

Let me be clear: I fail every single day. I'm not proud of that, but I'm not ashamed of it either.

There are times when I'm short-tempered with my kids. I've said things to my wife that I regretted. I've made bad calls in business. I've overlooked team members. I've spoken before I've listened. The list goes on.

But the goal isn't perfection. The goal is *progress.*

We need to kill this lie that strong leadership means getting it right all the time. It doesn't. Strong leadership means being willing to admit when you got it wrong, learn from it, and do better tomorrow.

It means being transparent with your team. Owning your mistakes. Letting people see that you're human, not invincible.

I call this **failing forward.** It's not just about falling—it's about the *direction* in which you fall. If you're going to fail (and you will), fail in the direction of growth. Let failure refine you, not define you.

TRAINING THE MINDSET OF RESILIENCE

Overcoming fear and failure isn't about one-time courage. It's about training a resilient mindset every single day.

That means:

- **Talking to yourself, not just listening to yourself.**
  - When fear starts whispering lies, you speak truth back to it. Declare God's promises. Remind yourself of your calling. Tell yourself who you are.

- **Surrounding yourself with people who challenge your thinking.**
    - Fear thrives in isolation. But when you're in community with other courageous people, their courage becomes contagious.
- **Normalizing failure in your culture.**
    - As a leader, the way you talk about failure matters. Celebrate smart risks, even when they don't work out. Create space for experimentation.
    - Let people know that mistakes are part of the growth process.
- **Practicing gratitude even when things go wrong.**
    - Gratitude rewires your brain. It helps you see the lesson in the loss, the beauty in the brokenness.

YOUR CALLING IS BIGGER THAN YOUR FEAR

This is personal for me. I believe each of us has a calling—a divine purpose placed in our lives by God. That calling isn't small. It's significant. And significant callings come with significant resistance.

The enemy of your soul will do everything possible to keep you stuck in fear. Why? Because he knows that your actions have the power to influence, to lead, to set others free.

When you shrink back, it doesn't just affect you. It affects everyone who was supposed to benefit from your leadership.

So the next time fear knocks, remember this: **Your calling is bigger than your fear.** Your purpose is more powerful than your doubt. And your future is worth fighting through every failure to reach.

FEAR IS A PROBLEM OF PERSPECTIVE

Fear often feels overwhelming because we see it through the wrong lens. We look at it up close, magnifying it until it becomes all we can see. But what if fear isn't the monster in the room—what if it's just a shadow cast by a misaligned perspective?

So much of fear is rooted in the *what ifs*: what if I fail, what if I'm rejected, what if it all falls apart? But rarely do we ask the equally powerful questions: What if I grow? What if I succeed? What if failure becomes the very thing that leads me to greater impact?

One of the people I most admire for his mindset around fear and failure is my good friend Nathan Cox. Nathan runs a highly successful real estate development company in south Alabama called 68 Ventures. He's built a powerhouse organization that has built thousands of homes, developed thousands of lots, led major infrastructure projects, and created opportunities across his region. But what impresses me most about Nathan isn't the scale of what he's built—it's the depth of his perspective.

Nathan once told me something that stuck with me like a tattoo on my mind. We were talking about risk, business cycles, and the fear that leaders carry when everything is on the line. He said:

> If I went bankrupt today—if it all collapsed—I would be *more valuable* to my next business partners, to my next venture, than I ever was before. Because I would have learned. I'd know what not to do. I'd know what to do. I'd have battle scars, but I'd also have wisdom. That kind of experience doesn't make you less—it makes you more.

Read that again.

That's not arrogance. That's clarity. That's a leader who understands that failure isn't the end of the road—it's part of the process. It's how you earn perspective you can't buy in a book or a seminar. It's how you gain the insight that sets the foundation for your next season.

Nathan's mindset reminds me that fear loses its grip when we zoom out. When we shift our view from the *moment* to the *mission*. From the failure to the *future*. What looks like a loss right now may turn out to be the exact catalyst God uses to equip you for something greater.

If you're paralyzed by fear, ask yourself: *What lens am I looking through?* Am I viewing failure as a death sentence, or as a detour toward growth? Am I defining myself by my setbacks, or refining myself through them?

Perspective doesn't eliminate fear, but it puts fear in its place. It shrinks it down to size. And it gives you the courage to move forward, even if the path is uncertain.

So what if you fall? What if it doesn't go according to plan? That's not the real fear. The real fear should be never trying—of never becoming who you were meant to be because you let a distorted perspective hold you back.

Take a page out of Nathan's book: Let failure educate you, not eliminate you. Let it make you stronger, wiser, and even more valuable to the world around you.

PUSH THROUGH

Overcoming fear and failure isn't a leadership *hack*. It's a leadership *habit*. It's the daily decision to rise above your doubts, to press on when things fall apart, and to lead with conviction even when your knees are shaking.

You're going to fail. You're going to feel fear. But you're also going to grow. You're going to inspire. You're going to build something that lasts because you were willing to lead through the fire.

> *Being confident of this, that he who began a good*
> *work in you will carry it on to completion.*
>
> —PHILIPPIANS 1:6 (NIV)

You don't push through on your own strength. Philippians 1:6 promises that "he who began a good work in you will carry it on to completion." Christ-centered leadership is about trusting that God Himself will finish what He started in you—even through your fear, even through your failure.

That's what leaders do. That's what *you* were built to do.

Key Highlights

- Failure isn't final—perseverance is the differentiator. Success comes not from avoiding failure but from pressing forward in the face of it.
- Breakthroughs often come from uncomfortable moments. Leaders who stretch themselves—even in fear—grow stronger. Action breaks fear's grip and turns failure into a stepping stone, not a stop sign.
- Resilient leaders develop habits: speaking truth over fear, learning from failure, surrounding themselves with courageous people, and choosing gratitude in difficulty. This daily mindset builds long-term strength.
- God-given purpose always outweighs fear. Scripture reminds leaders that their influence is divinely assigned, and setbacks are part of God's refining process—not signs to quit.

Reflection Questions

To close this chapter, let me leave you with a few practical ways to lead through fear and failure:

1. What are your top three limiting beliefs? Where did they come from? What can you replace them with?
2. What was your last failure? What did it teach you? How did it make you stronger?
3. What is something you consistently avoid doing because it makes you uncomfortable? What is one courageous act you can complete every week?

CHAPTER 7

THE COST OF LEADERSHIP

For everyone to whom much is given, from him much will be required.

—LUKE 12:48 (NKJV)

In January 1988, a catastrophic event unfolded at Ashland Oil's storage facility in Floreffe, Pennsylvania. A massive storage tank collapsed, releasing approximately 750,000 gallons of diesel fuel into the Monongahela River. This environmental disaster disrupted the drinking water supply for nearly a million residents across multiple states and led to extensive ecological damage.

At the helm of Ashland Oil was CEO John Hall. Confronted with this crisis, Hall chose a path of transparency and accountability. He promptly traveled to the spill site, held a press conference at which he took full responsibility for the incident, and assured the public that Ashland would cover all cleanup costs and compensate affected communities. Under his leadership, the company established a local claims office, provided alternative water supplies to impacted areas, and commissioned independent investigations to understand the spill's cause and prevent future occurrences.

Hall's decisive and empathetic response not only mitigated the immediate fallout but also set a precedent for corporate responsibility. His actions transformed a potential public relations disaster into a case study in effective crisis management, earning him recognition and restoring public trust in Ashland Oil.

Leadership often demands confronting unforeseen challenges head-on, making difficult decisions, and bearing the weight of responsibility not just for successes but also for failures.

There's a reason the majority of people in this world never fully step into the calling of leadership. And it's not because they lack talent, opportunity, or even desire. It's because they're not willing to pay the cost.

The hard truth is that real leadership demands more than most are willing to give. It's not glamorous. It's not always inspiring. In fact, it's often thankless, isolating and painful, and it requires more internal strength than any other role in life. That's why so few choose it. And why even fewer endure.

If you want to be great in life, if you want to lead people, influence culture, or build something meaningful, you must first understand this foundational truth: Leadership requires sacrifice.

THE LONELINESS OF LEADERSHIP

You've heard it said before: *It's lonely at the top.* But why is that true?

It's not because leaders don't have people around them. Most leaders are constantly surrounded by teams, family, employees, advisors, and even critics. No, it's lonely at the top because the weight of leadership is uniquely yours. When you lead, you bear the responsibility of direction, of vision, of consequence.

You can't lead everyone, and you certainly can't be everything to everyone. You only get 24 hours in a day, just like everyone else. That means you have to be ruthless with your priorities. For me, I've made peace with the fact that I'm not trying to be Elon Musk. I love what I do. I love building my company. I'm passionate about our mission, our people, and our growth. But I also love my family more. And I'm not willing to sacrifice dinners at home or bedtime stories with my kids just to chase an extra percentage of growth or one more deal.

Yes, that means my business might not scale at the same speed as someone who lives and breathes only business. But that's the cost I'm willing to pay. Leadership requires clarity about what matters most. And then, the courage to live aligned with those values, even when others might not understand.

OWNERSHIP AND BLAME

When things go wrong, the leader is the one who takes the fall. That's part of the job. And it's not optional.

You can't throw your team under the bus. You can't shift blame to a broken process or an underperforming department. If it happened on your watch, you own it. Period.

Great leaders absorb blame and deflect praise. They protect their team in public and correct them in private. That kind of leadership earns trust and builds culture. But it costs you your ego. It costs you the freedom to always be "right." And it requires thick skin because **the world has no shortage of critics.**

There will be people who question your decisions, doubt your motives, and criticize your results. And you have to be able to take that, not retaliate, and stay grounded in your identity and purpose. That's a cost many aren't willing to pay.

THE PAIN OF HARD CONVERSATIONS

One of the least discussed and most painful aspects of leadership is the need to have hard conversations. It's one thing to cast vision or celebrate wins. It's another to look someone in the eye and tell them they're not meeting the standard.

And at some point, if you're leading anything of significance, you're going to have to fire someone. Maybe even someone you like.

I'm a people person. I like almost everyone. I build relationships easily. I want people to win. But I've had to sit across the table from people I genuinely cared about and let them go, not because I wanted to, but because it was necessary. They weren't a fit, the organization was moving in a different direction, or we simply didn't have a role that matched their strengths.

These conversations are brutal. There have been tears. There's been cussing. There's been silence that speaks volumes. And every time, I carry it with me longer than I want to admit. But that's the cost of leadership. You don't get to outsource the hard calls. You don't get to avoid discomfort. Leadership means stepping into the mess and doing what needs to be done, even when it hurts.

UNPOPULAR BUT NECESSARY

There will be times when the right decision is not the popular one. As a leader, you'll be asked to make calls that disappoint your team, frustrate your family, or cause people to question your judgment.

You have to be okay with short-term disapproval in the service of long-term good. That means you'll go home some nights with a knot in your stomach, knowing that someone you care about is upset with you. That means you'll face moments where your principles are tested, where the easy road looks tempting, but you choose the hard road because it's the right one.

Here's how I think about it: if the decision isn't self-centered, and it's made for the good of the mission, the team, or the family, then I can live with the consequences. I can stomach the pushback. Because leadership isn't about pleasing people, it's about serving them. And sometimes, service requires short-term sacrifice for long-term flourishing.

Kirby Smart, head coach of the Georgia Bulldogs, gave a speech about the cost of leadership:

"You will have to make hard decisions that negatively affect people you care about … You will be disliked despite your best attempt to do the best for the most … You will be misunderstood and not always have the opportunity to defend yourself."

That's the emotional toll of leadership. Not just the strategic weight, but the relational cost too. You will be misunderstood, criticized, and at times, alone in your convictions. But that doesn't make you wrong. It just makes you responsible.

THE WEIGHT OF STRESS

Stress is a silent killer in leadership. And I'm not just talking about mental fatigue. I'm talking about the soul-crushing pressure of being the one responsible to make sure everything works for everyone.

When you're the leader, you carry the weight. You know what it's like to lie awake at night wondering if the cash flow will come through, if the client will sign, if the mistake can be fixed. You know what it's like to feel the unrelenting pressure to perform—not just for yourself, but for your team, your family, your investors, your customers.

And if you're not careful, it will consume you.

Growing up, I saw this firsthand. My dad was an incredibly hard worker. He loved what he did, and he built a strong reputation in the construction industry. But I watched him walk through one of the toughest chapters of his life when a major construction job went sideways. He ended up fighting a bogus lawsuit for years. He poured himself into the case, and he carried it like a personal betrayal.

It ate at him. Day and night, he obsessed over every detail. He stopped enjoying his work. The passion he once had for the industry slowly faded. That experience—watching the cost of leadership without the right boundaries or release—marked me. And it taught me that stress, unchecked, can take more than just your joy. It can steal your calling.

That's why I've learned to prioritize my own outlets. For me, it's prayer and exercise. Prayer realigns my soul. It reminds me that I'm not God—that I can trust Him with the outcomes. And exercise gives me a healthy outlet for the tension that builds up. You can't carry this weight alone. And you shouldn't.

As Philippians 4:6 (NLT) reminds us: "Don't worry about anything; instead, pray about everything. Tell God what you need, and thank him for all he has done."

NEVER STOP GROWING

Complacency is the death of leadership.

The world is constantly evolving. People are changing. Technology is shifting. Markets are dynamic. If you stop learning, you start losing. Leaders don't get the luxury of autopilot. They don't get to coast on past successes. The moment you stop growing is the moment you start falling behind.

Leadership is not a destination; it's a discipline. A lifestyle. A commitment to becoming better every single day. That's why I read. That's why I ask questions. That's why I stay curious.

And more than that, leadership requires modeling the behavior you want to see. You can't just delegate growth to your team. You have to be the example. How you show up matters. Your energy. Your discipline. Your consistency. Your humility. People are watching. And they don't follow your words—they follow your actions.

DELAYED GRATIFICATION

If you're in this for the quick win, leadership isn't for you.

Great leaders understand the power of delayed gratification. They sow seeds without demanding immediate harvest. They make investments that may not pay off for years. They build structures and culture and vision knowing that someone else might get the credit. But they do it anyway.

That's why I often reference the quote from Fabienne Fredrickson: "You don't eat the fruit from the seeds you plant today." It might take a season. It might take a decade. But the harvest will come—if you don't quit.

The problem is, we live in a world addicted to immediacy. We want results now. We want affirmation now. We want outcomes without the process. But leadership doesn't work that way.

You must be willing to work in silence, to sacrifice in obscurity, and to persevere through dry seasons. And along the way, you have to learn to celebrate small wins. Because if you're always waiting for the big breakthrough to feel fulfilled, you'll burn out before you get there.

DON'T QUIT

The cost of leadership is real. It's not a theory; it's a life you live. It's the sacrifices you make in the dark. It's a choice you make when no one is watching. It's the pressure you carry when everyone else goes home.

But it's worth it.

Because leadership is about purpose. It's about stewarding influence to serve others. It's about making the world better than you found it. It's about building something that outlives you.

And if you're called to it—if you believe you were born for this—then don't quit. Keep going. Keep growing. Keep sacrificing. Because the world needs more leaders who are willing to pay the price. Who are willing to carry the cost.

Because in the end, it's not about what you get from leadership. It's about who you become because of it.

Key Highlights

- True leadership demands far more than talent or desire—it requires personal cost, such as enduring criticism, making hard decisions, and putting mission over comfort or popularity.
- Leaders must take full responsibility for failures, have difficult conversations (including letting people go), and make unpopular decisions for the long-term good, even at emotional and relational expense.
- The weight of leadership is often isolating and stressful, requiring leaders to establish healthy outlets (like prayer or exercise) to avoid burnout and remain grounded in purpose.
- Complacency kills leadership. Growth must be intentional, modeled consistently, and rooted in a willingness to invest without immediate reward—understanding that leadership is a long game.
- Leadership isn't about what you get; it's about who you become. If you're called to lead, embrace the responsibility, endure the weight, and keep going—because your influence matters beyond yourself.

Reflection Questions

1. How do I respond when things go wrong? Do I deflect or take ownership?
2. Have I ever chosen the easy or popular path over the right one? What did it cost me?
3. In what areas of my leadership have I become complacent? In what areas have I been growing?

PART THREE
Leading Others with Purpose

CHAPTER 8

BUILDING TRUST AND INFLUENCE

Trust is the glue of life. It's the most essential ingredient in effective communication. It's the foundational principle that holds all relationships.

—STEPHEN COVEY

Every enduring relationship, thriving team, or lasting movement begins with one essential element: trust. Without it, leadership becomes shallow, influence is limited, and progress stalls. Trust is the soil in which all great leadership takes root. Influence is the fruit that grows from it.

Many leaders desire influence–the ability to inspire, guide, and shape outcomes at scale. But influence is not inherited or appointed. It is earned. And it is earned through trust. You can lead a few without trust for a while, but you will never lead many for long without it. Trust is the foundation; influence is the expansion. One allows you to lead with stability. The other enables you to lead with momentum.

As leaders, we don't stumble into trust. We build it intentionally. One decision, one action, one interaction at a time. The strongest leaders are not always the most charismatic or credentialed, but they are the most consistent. The most trusted. And from that trust flows lasting, multiplying influence.

Jesus modeled this masterfully. His influence didn't begin with crowds or miracles. It began with character and compassion. With the kind of presence that said, "You matter." He touched the untouchable, washed feet, served the marginalized, and sacrificed Himself. His trustworthiness transcended status. And because people trusted Him, they followed Him. Two thousand years later, His influence remains unmatched.

This chapter is about the kind of leadership that builds trust deeply and uses influence wisely. It is about becoming the kind of leader whose presence earns the right to be followed.

THE HIGH STAKES OF TRUST

Warren Buffett once said, "It takes 20 years to build a reputation and five minutes to ruin it." Few leaders have embodied this principle better than Tony Dungy, the legendary Super Bowl-winning NFL coach. Coaching at the highest level, he refused to compromise his values. He never shouted, belittled, or manipulated. He built a reputation of calm, faith-driven clarity. His players trusted him because he was consistent, humble, and principled, and that trust carried him all the way to a Super Bowl victory. His influence with his players lasted because of his character.

Your reputation is your relational currency. You can demand performance, manipulate outcomes, or purchase compliance, but you cannot buy trust. You must earn it through consistent integrity and selfless service. Proverbs 22:1 (ESV) puts it plainly: "A good name is to be chosen rather than great riches, and favor is better than silver or gold."

Trust begins with character, but it is upheld by clarity, consistency, and care. Leaders who protect trust create cultures of safety and confidence. They become anchors in uncertainty. And in a world of broken promises and shifting values, that kind of leadership stands out.

TEN PILLARS OF TRUSTWORTHY LEADERSHIP

Here are ten core principles that define leaders who build trust:

- **Authenticity**—They walk the talk. What you see is what you get.
- **Consistency**—They show up. They follow through.
- **Service**—They put others before themselves and champion the mission over their ego.
- **Integrity**—They do what is right, especially when it's costly.
- **Competence**—They deliver results and carry the weight of responsibility well.
- **Clarity**—They communicate honestly and frequently.
- **Empathy**—They listen, care, and make people feel seen.
- **Accountability**—They own their actions and create cultures of responsibility.
- **Faithfulness**—They stay committed, even when it's inconvenient.
- **Spiritual Grounding**—They lead from a place of dependence on God, not pride.

Proverbs 3:5–6 (NIV) reminds us, "Trust in the LORD with all your heart … and he will make your paths straight." Leaders who are grounded in something bigger than themselves lead with a steadiness that inspires trust.

FROM TRUST TO INFLUENCE

John C. Maxwell once said, "People buy into the leader before they buy into the vision." In other words, trust is the doorway to influence. Without trust, leadership becomes hollow—just a title without traction. But trust isn't the final destination; it's just the beginning. Influence is what you build once trust is established. And real influence? It's never about manipulation or control—it's about inspiration. It's about elevating others, equipping them, and empowering them to become more than they were yesterday.

Nelson Mandela's life is a striking example of trust turning into influence. After 27 years in prison, he had every reason to emerge bitter. Instead, he chose forgiveness and unity. That posture built trust not only with his allies but even with his former oppressors. Because he was trusted, his influence reached across political, racial, and cultural lines, helping to heal a divided nation.

In today's world, the word *influencer* has become a distorted version of its original meaning. Social media platforms have given rise to a generation of individuals labeled as "influencers," not because of the values they live by or the lives they change, but because of the attention they can attract. Influence today is often equated with visibility, popularity, or follower counts, but none of those things equate to real leadership or long-lasting impact.

Being someone of influence isn't a bad thing. In fact, it's a noble calling. But influence must be rooted in something deeper than curated photos and viral trends. True influence is not about being in the spotlight; it's about what you do with the light you've been given. Jesus said, "Let your light shine before others, that they may see your good deeds and glorify your Father in heaven" (Matthew 5:16 NIV). That's the heartbeat of real influence: using your platform not to elevate yourself, but to illuminate the path for others.

Influence is stewardship. It's a responsibility to lead with integrity, to speak with clarity, and to live with purpose. It means choosing impact over impression, legacy over likes, and faithfulness over fame. If your light shines but doesn't help others see more clearly, it's just a performance.

NINE WAYS TO CULTIVATE INFLUENCE THAT MULTIPLIES

1. **Lead Yourself First**—Be the kind of person you'd want to follow. Self-leadership is the foundation of all other leadership.
2. **Live with Conviction and Clarity**—Know your values, and don't compromise them. People follow clarity, not confusion.
3. **Serve Before You Speak**—Show up to serve, not to be seen. Influence flows from humility, not hype.
4. **Add Value Everywhere You Go**—Be a builder, not a consumer. Seek to leave every person, room, and conversation better than you found it.
5. **Be Consistent in Character**—Let who you are be your greatest credential. Integrity outlives charisma.
6. **Build Deep Relationships**—Prioritize people over projects. Influence grows in the soil of genuine connection.
7. **Lift Others as You Rise**—Leadership multiplies when shared. The true measure of your influence is the legacy you leave in others.
8. **Speak Life and Truth**—Be bold and hopeful in your communication. Words carry weight—use them wisely.
9. **Model Excellence in the Small Things**—Greatness begins in obscurity. Faithfulness in little builds capacity for more.

Luke 16:10 (NIV) reminds us, "Whoever can be trusted with very little can also be trusted with much." Great influence isn't built on grand stages or viral moments—it's built on the small, daily decisions to lead with integrity and purpose, even when no one is watching.

STAY REAL

Craig Groeschel once said, "People would rather follow a leader who is always real than one who is always right." It's a powerful reminder that leadership is not about having all the answers; rather, it's about showing up and putting your best foot forward for others every day. In a world full of filters, facades, and curated personas, what people are truly craving is *realness*. Authenticity beats polish. Integrity outweighs image. And trust will always outlast charisma.

You don't need a microphone or a title to lead. You don't need a stage or a social media following. What you need is a life worth following. A life that's lived with conviction, consistency, and character. Leadership isn't reserved for those in high positions; it's practiced daily in the quiet decisions, the difficult conversations, the unseen sacrifices, and the courageous choices to do the right thing when no one is watching.

The most impactful leaders aren't the ones chasing influence; they're the ones faithfully stewarding it. They lead not for applause, but out of purpose. They don't just cast vision; they *live* it. They earn trust not through perfection, but through their presence, their transparency, and their commitment to walk alongside those they lead.

So build trust with intention. Show up, even when it's inconvenient. Own your mistakes. Celebrate others. Keep your word. Make the kind of decisions that your future self (and your future team) will be proud of.

Steward your influence with humility. Influence isn't about being the center of attention; it's about lifting others into the light. When leadership becomes less about ego and more about others, it starts to reflect the kind of servant-hearted leadership Jesus modeled.

Let your leadership be a light that others can walk by—not a spotlight that blinds them, but a steady flame that offers warmth, guidance, and hope.

That is how trust is built.

That is how influence grows.

That is how leaders are built to lead.

Key Highlights

- Leadership that lasts is rooted in trust, not charisma or authority. Trust is earned over time through consistent character, and influence flows naturally from that foundation.
- Trustworthy leaders are authentic, consistent, humble, and grounded in purpose. Their presence—not their platform—earns them the right to lead.
- True influence is about service, not self-promotion. It's measured by impact, not impression—by how well you elevate others, not by how many eyes are on you.
- Integrity in the unseen moments—keeping your word, leading yourself first, lifting others as you rise—is what qualifies a person for greater influence.
- In a filtered world, people crave realness. Leaders who are vulnerable, principled, and people-first will outlast those chasing titles or fame.

Reflection Questions

1. Do the people closest to you—your family, team, or peers—see you as a trustworthy leader? What evidence supports your answer?
2. Do your actions consistently reflect your values even when no one is watching? Where might there be a gap between what you say and what you do?
3. How are you building trust with your team on a daily basis? What small habits reinforce your integrity, presence, and reliability?

CHAPTER 9

COMMUNICATION THAT MOVES PEOPLE

*The art of communication
is the language of leadership.*

—Dr. Martin Luther King Jr.

In the realm of leadership, communication is the very bridge between vision and execution, between inspiration and action. Words carry weight. Presence carries power. And how we engage with those we lead determines whether they simply follow orders or follow us with their hearts.

John D. Rockefeller built one of the most powerful business empires the world has ever known. He was a titan of industry, a pioneer of the modern corporation, and at one point, the wealthiest man alive. But those who knew him best rarely spoke of his wealth or ruthlessness first. What they remembered most was how he communicated.

He never shouted. Not once. In boardrooms filled with tension, in negotiations worth millions, in the face of chaos, Rockefeller remained calm. He spoke with clarity, not volume. His tone was measured. His words were carefully chosen. There was power in his restraint. And in that stillness, he commanded attention.

In today's culture, where loudness is often mistaken for leadership, Rockefeller's approach offers a striking contrast. Real authority doesn't have to raise its voice. It invites, it influences, it inspires.

So what made his communication effective?

- **Self-control signaled steadiness, not stress.** His composure gave people confidence.
- **Pause and reflection before speaking.** He didn't fill the silence with noise. He allowed thoughts to breathe.
- **Emotional consistency builds trust.** People knew what to expect—no mood swings, no outbursts.
- **Quiet competence commanded attention.** The less he said, the more others leaned in to hear.

Rockefeller reminds us that true leadership communicates not to dominate, but to dignify. Not to demand, but to draw people in. It's an art that speaks not just to the mind, but also to the heart.

Fast-forward to 2006. Ford Motor Company was in trouble. Decades of decline had brought the American giant to its knees. Billions were being lost. Executive meetings were filled with green status reports pretending everything was fine.

Then came a turning point.

Mark Fields, President of Ford Americas, dared to break the silence. During a weekly Business Plan Review (BPR) meeting, he presented a red slide admitting a serious problem. The room tensed. No one knew how new CEO Alan Mulally would respond.

Mulally paused.

Then he simply said:

"Mark, that's great visibility. That's what we need. Who can help Mark with this?"

That moment changed everything. In a culture plagued by fear and false harmony, Mulally praised honesty instead of punishing it. He set a new tone of trust, transparency, and team.

What made Mulally different?

- **Psychological safety:** He created a space where truth could be spoken without fear.
- **Humility and curiosity:** He asked questions instead of assigning blame.
- **Consistent clarity:** His mantra of "One Ford. One Team. One Plan. One Goal" brought alignment and purpose.
- **Communication rhythm:** The weekly BPRs became sacred. Not a formality, but a rhythm of accountability, honesty, and hope.

Ford didn't turn around because of a spreadsheet. It turned around because of a sentence. Because leadership is communication, and communication shapes culture.

A CONFESSION OF PRESENCE

I want to be someone who speaks life into others. I want to lead in a way that builds people up, not just through my words but through my presence, too. But if I'm honest, this is an area I'm constantly working on. Leadership has stretched me, challenged me, and exposed blind spots I didn't know I had. And one of the biggest? How easily I can be physically present, but emotionally absent.

There are moments (more than I'd like to admit) when I'm deep in the zone. I'm locked in, tunnel-visioned, driven by the weight of the vision I carry. I'm chasing the next solution, fighting fires, strategizing, creating. And then, someone walks into my office. A teammate, a partner, maybe even a friend. They step into the room needing something—time, direction, encouragement, clarity. But at that moment, it feels like a disruption. I don't mean for it to be. I'm not angry. I'm not annoyed. I'm just consumed. But the message I send is clear: Not now. Not you. Not important.

And that realization stings.

Because I know what it's like to feel unseen. I know what it's like to walk away from an interaction feeling dismissed. And if I'm not careful, I become the kind of leader I never wanted to be—too busy for people. Too focused on goals to see the gold in others. Too driven by the next step to notice that the person standing right in front of me is most likely the answer to whatever "problem" I'm trying to solve.

But here's what I've learned, and what I'm still learning every day: People aren't interruptions. They're the reason I lead. Vision is important. Goals matter. But the people—*they* are the mission. The culture I long to create and the legacy I hope to leave—they're all built on relationships. Leadership, at its core, is about serving people well. And I can't serve what I don't see.

Presence is powerful. It's not about being in the room; it's about being *with* the room. People can feel the difference. They can tell when you're fully there versus when you're just going through the motions. True presence isn't something you can fake. It's felt. And it speaks louder than words.

In fact, communication is always happening—even in silence. It's not just the words we use; it's the tone of our voice, the direction of our gaze, the position of our body. It's the sighs, the pauses, the nods—or lack thereof. It's the moment someone walks in and we either turn toward them or keep our eyes glued to the screen. We are always communicating something, even when we're not saying anything at all.

And if we're not careful, our silence can speak of rejection. Our distracted posture can send a message of disinterest. Our busyness can unintentionally broadcast that people are a nuisance instead of a priority. That's not who I want to be. That's not how I want to lead.

I've had to ask God to help me slow down. Not just externally, but internally. I've had to pray for margin—not just in my schedule, but in my soul. Because it's not enough to be available in body. I want to be available in spirit. I want to be the kind of leader who makes people feel seen and safe. Who listens with his eyes as well as his ears. Who communicates worth before he communicates instruction.

I've asked God to help me see people the way He does—not as interruptions to my productivity, but as sacred opportunities to reflect His love. Because the truth is, behind every request, every question, every pop-in conversation is a person carrying weight I may never see. And sometimes, what they need most isn't a solution—it's my attention. My eye contact. My care. *My presence.*

There's a unique responsibility that comes with leadership: People read you even when you're not speaking. They pick up on your energy, your mood, your posture. Your team often draws more meaning from how you show up than from what you say. That's why your presence matters even more than your position. You can have the title, the authority, the experience, but if your presence is cold, detached, or distracted, the people around you won't feel led. They'll feel managed.

And no one wants to be managed. They want to be *known.*

I've had to learn that presence isn't something you master once. It's a discipline. A daily decision. It means pausing when everything in you wants to press forward. It means turning your chair, looking someone in the eyes, and engaging with your full attention, even if it's just for a few minutes. It means remembering that the person in front of you isn't in the way of the mission—they *are* the mission.

There have been times when someone walked into my office and I almost brushed them off. But by God's grace, I paused. I listened. And what started as a quick question turned into a deep, meaningful moment—a breakthrough, a revelation, a chance to encourage someone on the edge of burnout. Moments like that remind me: Ministry isn't always scheduled. Leadership isn't always convenient. And some of the most important things you'll do as a leader won't show up on your to-do list.

Presence costs you something. It costs your focus, your time, your comfort. But it's worth everything. Because the more present you are, the more influence you have. Not through pressure or position, but through connection. Presence is what earns trust. It's what builds culture. It's what turns ordinary moments into transformational ones.

And when presence becomes your default posture—not just in the big moments but in the daily ones too—everything changes. Your team feels it. Your family feels it. You feel it. The atmosphere shifts. And leadership stops being about what you do and starts being about who you are.

So I keep asking God to help me lead like Jesus—fully present, deeply aware, and always available to love. Because in the end, the greatest leaders aren't remembered for how fast they moved or how much they achieved. They're remembered for how they made people feel. And that begins with presence.

Because your presence communicates more than your position ever will.

THE POWER AND WEIGHT OF WORDS

Maya Angelou said it best:

> *People will forget what you said, people will forget what you did, but people will never forget how you made them feel.*

That truth has echoed in my leadership journey more times than I can count. Because at the end of the day, communication isn't just about the content of our message—it's about the *impact* of our presence. Great communication doesn't merely inform. It transforms. It doesn't just fill the air with sound; it leaves a mark on the soul.

Your words carry emotional weight. They can be a spark that ignites belief or a shadow that dims confidence. They can lift someone out of discouragement or reinforce the lies they're already telling themselves. And as a leader, your words are multiplied. Magnified. They echo longer and louder than you realize.

When you walk into a room, your energy often speaks before your mouth does. The question is, what does it say? Are you bringing hope, or heaviness? Light, or tension? Encouragement, or critique?

Smile. Encourage. Celebrate wins—big and small. Speak life into people, not just about people.

Don't underestimate the power of small, sincere words:

"I'm proud of you."
"I noticed the effort you gave."
"You bring something special to this team."

Leadership isn't just about giving direction—it's about shaping the atmosphere. And few things shape culture more than the words leaders choose to speak. Encouragement costs nothing, but it deposits something priceless. When given sincerely and consistently, it becomes fuel—fuel for morale, for motivation, and for movement.

But it's not just what you say—it's how you say it. Proverbs 18:21 (NIV) reminds us:

"The tongue has the power of life and death."

Words are seeds. They're planting something every time they're spoken. Are you sowing confidence or confusion? Clarity or criticism? Hope or hesitation? Because whatever you plant, it will grow.

In the early years of my leadership, I didn't always filter my words. If I felt something, I said it. Raw, uncut, unfiltered. I prided myself on being honest and direct—on keeping it real. But what I didn't realize was that being "real" without wisdom can cause real damage. Honesty without love isn't leadership—it's recklessness.

Just because it's true doesn't mean it needs to be said.

And even if it does, *how* it's said often matters just as much as *what* is said.

That realization led me to adopt a personal filter—one I still use today. Before I speak, I ask:

- Is this helpful?
- Is this the right time?
- Is this the right tone?
- Have I really thought this through?

I've learned that silence is better than careless truth. And wisdom often shows up not in how much you speak, but in what you choose not to say.

James 1:19 (NIV) offers timeless guidance:

"Everyone should be quick to listen, slow to speak and slow to become angry."

That's not passivity—it's leadership maturity. Intentional words aren't fake; they're responsible. They recognize that every sentence shapes something. And as a leader, people are listening closely— often more closely than you think. What you say on your worst day can become someone else's narrative for years. What you speak in a moment of frustration might take months to undo.

So choose wisely. Speak with clarity, with purpose, with life. Your words are either building a culture where people flourish—or one where they fear. You get to decide.

Because in the end, the most powerful leaders aren't the ones with the best speeches. They're the ones whose words make people feel stronger, not smaller. Seen, not overlooked. Empowered, not intimidated.

That's the weight of your words. And that's the opportunity of leadership.

THE LEADERSHIP POWER OF LISTENING

If words are the engine of communication, then listening is the steering wheel. It guides the conversation. It shapes understanding. And it determines whether your words actually take people anywhere— or just make noise.

In a world full of voices competing to be heard, leaders who *listen* stand out.

Stephen Covey famously said:

"Seek first to understand, then to be understood."

That single principle could transform most teams, marriages, partnerships, and organizations. But here's the challenge: Listening is hard. It requires humility. It demands presence. It means putting your own agenda on pause long enough to truly hear the heart of someone else.

Most people don't listen with the intent to understand—they listen with the intent to reply. They're simply waiting for their turn to talk. You can see it in their eyes—they've already moved on to formulating their response. But leadership calls us higher. It calls us to tune in, to lean in, to listen not just with our ears but with our hearts.

Listening is leadership.

Active listening isn't passive. It's intentional. It's sacrificial. It means setting your phone down, turning away from the screen, making eye contact, and being *fully there* in the moment.

When you truly listen to someone, you're telling them:

"You matter. You're seen. You're heard."

And in that space, trust begins to grow.

In my experience, some of the most powerful moments in leadership have had nothing to do with the words I said, and everything to do with the silence I offered. Just being present. Just *listening*. Sometimes, people don't need a quick answer. They don't need you to fix it. They just need to be heard. They need to process it out loud. They need a safe space to speak freely.

And when you create that space as a leader, something sacred happens: Walls come down. Hearts open. Loyalty is built. And solutions often rise from the very person who just needed time to be understood.

Proverbs 18:13 (NIV) offers this warning:

"To answer before listening—that is folly and shame."

How often have we done exactly that? Rushed into problem-solving mode before understanding the problem. Assumed someone's motives before hearing their story. Cut people off because we were too busy—or too proud—to really listen.

But when we answer before listening, we rob ourselves of wisdom. We sabotage connection. We miss what's actually going on beneath the surface.

Listening is one of the simplest ways to show honor. It says, "You matter more than this moment. Your perspective is worth hearing, even if I don't agree with it. I care more about who you are than how fast we can move past this."

It also helps us become more discerning leaders. When you listen well, you hear not just what's being said—but what's not being said. You pick up on tone. On hesitations. On the emotional undercurrents. And that kind of awareness can help you lead with greater empathy and precision.

But here's the key: You have to slow down.

You can't listen in a hurry. You can't be present while multitasking. True listening happens at the speed of relationship—not at the speed of efficiency.

So pause. Ask questions. Let silence breathe. Nod. Reflect back what you heard to show understanding. And when needed, resist the urge to jump in with a solution. Sometimes your silence *is* the solution. Sometimes what people need most isn't your advice—it's your attention.

If you want to lead well, listen deeply.

If you want to influence, listen first.

If you want to build a culture of trust, start by modeling what it looks like to care enough to hear.

Because listening isn't just polite—it's powerful.

It's not soft; it's strategic.

It's not weakness; it's wisdom.

And the leaders who move people the most are often the ones who talk less and listen more.

ASK GREAT QUESTIONS

Leaders aren't just great speakers. They're great question-askers. Jesus modeled this beautifully. He didn't just lecture—He invited people into discovery. His questions weren't surface. They went straight to the heart.

Here are a few that have shaped my own leadership:

- What's the real challenge you're facing?
- How did that make you feel?
- What's something you're not saying, but wish you could?

These questions open people up. They go beyond facts and into feelings. Beyond the surface and into the soul. And they're how leaders lead with compassion.

FEEDBACK, CLARITY, AND THE COURAGE TO BE HONEST

Leadership without clarity is chaos. When direction is vague, expectations are unclear, and communication is inconsistent, people don't grow—they drift. Confusion corrodes momentum. Silence breeds assumptions. And in the absence of clarity, culture begins to fracture.

People don't rise to the level of our vision—they rise to the level of our *clarity*. If we want our teams to thrive, we must lead with precision. We must be willing to speak the truth in love, to offer feedback that fuels growth, and to step into uncomfortable conversations with courage.

Proverbs 27:6 (NIV) offers a sobering reminder:

"Wounds from a friend can be trusted, but an enemy multiplies kisses."

That verse flips modern leadership on its head. In a culture obsessed with comfort and approval, Scripture invites us to a deeper kind of love—one that dares to tell the truth, even when it's hard.

Because real love doesn't flatter. It sharpens. And the leaders who leave the deepest impact aren't always the nicest in the moment; they're the ones who care enough to be honest.

FEEDBACK IS A GIFT

Feedback is not cruelty. Done right, it's one of the most powerful expressions of leadership love. When you give someone thoughtful, constructive, well-timed feedback, what you're really saying is, "I believe in you. I see something greater inside you than what you're currently displaying."

That's not criticism—it's belief.

But like any powerful tool, feedback must be wielded with care. Otherwise, it can do more harm than good. Poorly delivered feedback can crush confidence, sow resentment, or spark confusion. That's why effective feedback is always:

- **Specific.** Vague feedback doesn't help anyone. "Do better" isn't a strategy. Tell them what worked, what didn't, and why.
- **Timely.** Don't wait until review season. Feedback delayed becomes feedback diluted. The longer you wait, the less impact it has.
- **Anchored in values.** Tie feedback to your mission, your shared goals, and your core values. Make it about growth, not just correction.

When feedback flows from a place of care and alignment, it builds trust. It becomes less about fault-finding and more about future-building.

RECEIVE IT WITH HUMILITY

Feedback is a two-way street. If you want a culture of truth, it starts with you. You must *model* what it looks like to receive feedback without getting defensive, dismissive, or disengaged.

That's easier said than done.

There have been times I've received feedback that stung, sometimes because it was poorly delivered, other times because it hit a nerve. But I've learned to pause, breathe, and say thank you. Not because it feels good, but because it's *good for me*. And every time I respond with humility, I reinforce a culture of openness.

If your team (or family) doesn't feel safe giving you feedback, they'll stop being honest. And when people stop being honest with you, you're no longer leading—you're being humored.

Great leaders don't just give feedback. They invite it. They create space for it. They welcome it as a tool for growth, not an attack on identity.

CLARITY BUILDS CULTURE

In 1 Corinthians 14:8 (NIV), Paul says:

> "If the trumpet does not sound a clear call, who will get ready for battle?"

Leadership is the trumpet. And your job is to sound a call that's unmistakable.

Don't assume your people know what's expected. Spell it out. Repeat it. Reinforce it. Vision leaks. Expectations drift. Clarity must be repeated until it echoes.

You cannot hold people accountable for what you haven't made clear. That's not leadership; that's a setup for frustration. If you're frustrated with someone on your team, ask yourself: *Did I clearly define what success looks like for them? Did I explain the "why" behind the what?*

People want to win. But you have to show them what winning looks like. Clarity doesn't just drive performance; it also cultivates peace. When people know where they stand and what's expected, they operate with more confidence, creativity, and freedom.

COURAGEOUS CONVERSATIONS

This is one area I've had to be very intentional about improving. There's no way around it—leadership requires hard conversations. And often, the conversations we avoid are the ones most needed.

We fear hurting feelings. We fear the reaction. We fear being misunderstood. So we wait. We soften. We water down the truth until it loses all power. But here's what I've learned: *Avoiding conflict doesn't preserve relationships—it weakens them.* What you tolerate today becomes your culture tomorrow.

Hard conversations are sacred ground. They test your maturity, your tone, your heart. But they also build the deepest trust when done with grace and truth. When your team sees that you care enough to tell the truth and are skilled enough to do it kindly, you earn credibility that no motivational speech can match.

Lead the conversations you dread. Don't delay what love demands.

Start with questions. Listen with empathy. Speak with compassion. And anchor everything in truth and mission. Your people will feel the difference.

And remember, your team is watching—not just what you say, but *how* you say it. They're watching how you handle tension. How you course-correct. And those moments shape the emotional temperature of your culture far more than your most inspirational moments ever will.

COMMUNICATION THAT MOVES PEOPLE

In the end, leadership is not just about what you build, but about how you speak, how you listen, and how you make people feel along the way. Words are tools, but presence is power. Listening is love. Clarity is kindness. And courage is the willingness to speak the truth even when it's hard.

The leaders who move people the most aren't always the loudest or the most eloquent. They're the ones whose presence brings peace.

Whose words bring life. Whose posture says, "You matter." They don't just communicate to direct—they communicate to *connect*.

Great communication is never just about transferring information. It's about transformation. It's about helping people feel seen, heard, and valued in a world that constantly rushes past them.

So may your leadership not be measured by how much you say, but by how deeply others feel seen in your presence. May your voice bring clarity, your silence bring safety, and your words plant seeds that grow into confidence, alignment, and trust.

Because when you communicate with intentionality, integrity, and heart—you don't just inform people; **you move them.**

Key Highlights

- Being fully engaged—not just physically present—builds trust and connection.
- Words can shape culture. How and what you communicate impacts morale, clarity, and momentum.
- Leaders who truly listen create safety, connection, and deeper influence.
- Clarity is kindness. Clear expectations, honest feedback, and courageous conversations drive growth.
- Strive for connection, not control. Great leadership communication inspires, encourages, and moves people forward.

Reflection Questions

1. Am I fully present with the people I lead, or am I merely physically available but mentally elsewhere? What does my body language communicate when someone walks into the room?
2. Do I listen with the intent to understand, or just to respond? How often do I truly *hear* the people around me before I speak?
3. What kind of communication culture am I modeling in my team, my home, or my business? Is it one of fear and confusion, or one of honesty, grace, and growth?

CHAPTER 10

RELATIONSHIPS RUN THE WORLD

The most important single ingredient in the formula of success is knowing how to get along with people.

—THEODORE ROOSEVELT

Leadership is built on relationships. Period. You can have the greatest vision, the most polished strategy, or the strongest skill set, but if you can't connect with people, you won't go far. Relationships are the glue that holds teams together, the bridge that carries influence, and the engine that drives every great mission forward.

Scripture reinforces this truth over and over again:

Be devoted to one another in love. Honor one another above yourselves.

—ROMANS 12:10 (NIV)

Do nothing out of selfish ambition or vain conceit.
Rather, in humility value others above yourselves.

—Philippians 2:3 (NIV)

Whether you're leading at work, leading in your home, or leading within your community, the way you relate to people determines the depth of your leadership.

Jesus didn't build His ministry on a platform or in a palace. He built it around a table. He spent three years walking with, eating with, and investing deeply in a small group of disciples. Jesus didn't just teach His disciples; He invited them into His life. He corrected them, encouraged them, forgave them, and gave them responsibility before they were ready. That raises a question every leader should ask: **Whom do I trust to speak truthfully into my life, even when it's uncomfortable?**

Out of that group came a movement that would change the course of human history. Discipleship, transformation through relationship, is still the most powerful leadership model the world has ever seen.

Nick Saban didn't just build a football dynasty at Alabama through elite recruiting and smart playbooks. He did it through intentional, relational mentorship. His coaching "tree" includes names like Kirby Smart, Lane Kiffin, Dan Lanning, Mario Cristobal, Jimbo Fisher, and many other successful head coaches.

Saban invested deeply in his assistants, holding them to high standards while also equipping them for future leadership. Even after they moved on, they credited their success to his influence.

Great leaders raise other leaders by giving them access and by inviting their perspective. As you build relationships in your circle, ask: **Who has experience or spiritual maturity that I lack?** If you can't point to someone, it may be time to pursue a mentor, coach, or guide who can stretch you.

Warren Buffett and Charlie Munger are icons not just for their investing genius but also for the *relationship* that powered it. For over 50 years, they led Berkshire Hathaway with unwavering loyalty and trust. They never tried to outshine each other. Instead, they complemented each other's strengths, sharpened each other's thinking, and built a legacy together:

> *Charlie and I never had an argument in all those years. When you have that kind of relationship, you can move mountains.*
>
> —WARREN BUFFETT

Long-term partnership outperforms short-term brilliance. Deep relationships create stability that money can't buy.

HOW DO YOU BUILD GREAT RELATIONSHIPS?

Real, meaningful relationships don't happen by accident. They take time, trust, and intentional investment. Think about marriage. Parenting. Deep friendships. These aren't built on convenience—they're built on consistency.

The same goes for leadership. Whether at home or at work, the principles are the same:

- **Serve others.** Put their needs before your own.
- **Add value.** Look for ways to enrich their lives.
- **Be present.** Show up fully—physically, emotionally, and mentally.
- **Be consistent.** Trust is built on repetition.

Whether you're leading at home or in the workplace, the principles remain the same. The application may differ—at work, you may lead with performance goals; at home, with patience and tenderness—but in both spaces, what people ultimately need is your attention, your belief, and your presence.

RETURN ON RELATIONSHIPS

One of my good friends, Austin Tenpenny, introduced me to a phrase I've never forgotten: **Return on relationships.** Most leaders are obsessed with ROI—Return on investment. They measure value in numbers, spreadsheets, and outcomes. But the greatest and most enduring impact often comes through **ROR—Return on relationships.** Influence, loyalty, innovation, and culture are all *relational dividends.* The deeper the trust, the stronger the team.

Because here's the truth: Vision gets traction through people. Strategy comes alive through people. Innovation, creativity, loyalty, momentum—it all flows through people. When you invest deeply in relationships, you begin to see dividends that no balance sheet can measure.

You'll see:

- **Influence:** People don't just listen because of your title; they follow because of your trust.
- **Loyalty:** Trust breeds commitment. When people know you care, they'll go further than you imagined.
- **Collaboration:** Strong relationships break down silos. Teams begin to share, support, and synergize.
- **Resilience:** When times get hard (and they always eventually do) relational trust holds the foundation in place.

Dale Carnegie captured this beautifully in *How to Win Friends and Influence People.* His principles weren't gimmicks; they were wisdom:

- Remember names.
- Smile sincerely.
- Take interest in people's stories.
- Give genuine praise.
- Let others talk more than you do.

These may sound simple, but simple doesn't mean shallow. Sometimes, it's the simplest relational disciplines that leave the deepest marks.

YOUR GREATEST CONTRIBUTION MIGHT BE A PERSON

Andy Stanley once said:

Your greatest contribution to the kingdom of God may not be something you do, but someone you raise.

That hits deep. And it should. Because the true weight of your legacy will never be measured in numbers, awards, or titles. It will be measured in people.

Not the ones who applauded you from afar, but the ones you walked with up close. The leaders you developed. The children you nurtured. The spouse you loved well. The friend you stood by in their lowest valley. The teammate you believed in when no one else would. Those people are the fingerprints of your legacy.

I have no greater joy than to hear that my children are walking in the truth.

—3 John 4 (NIV)

Legacy isn't just the story you tell—it's the story others will tell *because* of you. And more often than not, that story will have a face, not a statistic.

THE MYTH OF BIG IMPACT

We live in a culture that idolizes visibility. If it's not posted, praised, or platformed, we assume it doesn't matter. But that's not how the Kingdom works.

Some of the most world-changing leaders were raised in obscurity. David was tending sheep when God found him. Timothy was a young man being mentored by Paul. Ruth stayed faithful in the fields long before she stepped into legacy.

Impact isn't always loud. Sometimes, it's quiet. Personal. Hidden. But powerful.

That quiet cup of coffee with a struggling team member? That late-night talk with your teenager? That steady coaching of someone who's still rough around the edges?

Those moments might be your most eternal contributions.

You might not change the world through what you build. You might change the world through *who* you build.

FROM SUCCESS TO SIGNIFICANCE

There's a difference between success and significance:

- **Success** is what you achieve.
- **Significance** is what you sow into others.

One fades with time. The other multiplies beyond your lifetime.

You don't have to be the hero of every story. In fact, your greatest power may lie in being the guide—the one who unlocks potential in someone else. The mentor who creates margin for a younger leader to shine. The boss who gives a second chance instead of a final warning. The parent who blesses rather than criticizes.

Great leaders don't just make a name. They make disciples.

Just look at Jesus. His greatest legacy wasn't the sermons or the miracles—it was the 12 ragtag men He poured into, who went on to carry the message to the ends of the Earth. He invested deeply in people, and through them, the world was changed.

LIVE IN A WAY THAT ECHOES

At the end of your life, no one will ask how many awards you won or how many followers you had.

They'll ask:

- Did you love well?
- Did you listen?

- Did you believe in people?
- Did you walk humbly?
- Did you pour yourself out for others?

Because when it's all said and done, your name won't live on in stone—it will live on in stories. In the grateful prayers of a former employee. In the strength of a child raised in love. In the courage of a young leader who remembers, *"She believed in me when I couldn't believe in myself."*

THE REAL LEADERSHIP QUESTION

So the real question isn't *What am I building?*

It's *Who am I building?*

Are you investing in the relationships that matter most?

Are you showing up with humility, consistency, and vision?

Are you raising up others—or just raising up your own brand?

Because leadership isn't about building a platform. It's about building people.

And the ones who do that best? They're the ones who truly change the world.

Legacy is not something you leave behind.

Legacy is someone you *send forward*.

THE CIRCLE AUDIT

Your relationships shape your direction. Period.

You don't become the person God has called you to be in isolation—you get there with the help, encouragement, sharpening, and support of others. But not *everyone* in your life plays the same role, and not everyone is meant to walk the entire journey with you. My coach, Trevor McGregor, says it this way: "Some people are in your life for a reason, some for a season, and some for a lifetime." That's why every great leader must regularly take stock of their relational ecosystem.

Every 90 days, do a Circle Audit. Ask yourself:

- **Who's sharpening me?** Who challenges me to grow? Who speaks truth into my blind spots and pulls the best out of me?
- **Who's draining me?** Who consistently pulls me into drama, distraction, or discouragement? Who demands my energy but never multiplies it?
- **Who needs more of me?** Who's hungry to grow? Who's faithful and available but underinvested in? Who's waiting for me to reach out and lead them?
- **Who needs less of me?** Not out of judgment, but because their season in my inner circle may be shifting or because their voice is no longer aligned with my direction.

This isn't about coldly cutting people out—it's about being *intentional*. Jesus loved the world, taught the multitudes, and healed the crowds, but He didn't give everyone equal access.

- He had the **crowd**—the curious, the needy, the hungry.
- He had the **72**—faithful followers sent on mission.
- He had the **12**—disciples who walked closely with Him.
- And He had the **3**—Peter, James, and John—who saw His transfiguration, His agony, and His miracles up close.

Even Jesus, the Son of God, stewarded His proximity with purpose. He didn't apologize for that. He didn't try to be equally available to everyone. He knew His assignment, and He knew who was meant to walk closest with Him to fulfill it.

And so should you.

Many leaders confuse kindness with access. You can love people without inviting them into your inner circle. You can serve them without giving them your attention 24/7. You can honor someone's humanity without letting them shape your decisions.

Why? Because proximity has power. The people who are closest to you shape so much of you: your mindset, habits, standards, pace, future, words … The list goes on and on.

You can't afford to delegate that influence casually. If you're constantly being drained, distracted, or discouraged by the voices in your inner circle, it won't be long before your leadership starts to unravel. On the flip side, when you're surrounded by faith-filled, mission-minded, wise and honest people—your capacity multiplies. You begin to grow faster, lead stronger, and endure longer.

THE FIVE VOICES OF THE INNER CIRCLE

As you do your Circle Audit, pay attention to the *voices* in your life. One person may carry more than one voice, but in my experience, every leader needs these five voices in their life:

1. **The Coach**—Someone who pushes you to improve and doesn't accept your excuses.
2. **The Encourager**—Someone who reminds you of who you are on hard days.
3. **The Challenger**—Someone who asks the uncomfortable questions and sharpens your thinking.
4. **The Listener**—Someone who doesn't rush to fix but is a safe space for your processing.
5. **The Protégé**—Someone you're pouring into consistently, who multiplies your leadership downstream.

If your circle is full of people who only take or only agree with you—you're vulnerable. Audit the balance. Be intentional about developing a circle that *gives*, not just one that *demands*.

One of the most powerful things a leader can do is give themselves **permission to adjust the access levels** in their life.

- You're not obligated to stay close to people who keep sabotaging your peace.

- You're not called to carry everyone who refuses to grow.
- You're not failing anyone by moving from "constant avail-ability" to "healthy boundaries."

You can't lead others well if you're emotionally exhausted all the time.

When you adjust your circle with prayer, humility, and clarity, you're not being selfish—you're being a good steward of the calling God's placed on your life.

DIRECTION REQUIRES DISCERNMENT

Your destiny is too important to delegate your inner circle to chance.

Build your circle with purpose. I love sports, so I think about my circle like I'm trying to build a team that is going to win a championship. You wouldn't put just anyone in the game—you'd choose people who understand the mission, respect the process, and bring out the best in one another.

Be friendly with all, but build intimately with the faithful. The people around you are either pulling you toward God's best or pulling you away from it. So audit your circle, not out of arrogance, but for alignment.

Your future is too valuable to leave this to default.

SEEKING WISE COUNSEL

No leader can see everything clearly. No matter how gifted, visionary, or experienced you are, there will always be blind spots—areas where your emotions, assumptions, or limited vantage point cloud your judgment. That's why wise counsel isn't optional for a great leader—it's essential.

> *Plans fail for lack of counsel, but with many*
> *advisers they succeed.*

—PROVERBS 15:22 (NIV)

*Listen to advice and accept discipline, and at the
end you will be counted among the wise.*

—PROVERBS 19:20 (NIV)

Throughout Scripture, wisdom is consistently tied to relationships. The fool isolates himself and trusts only his own perspective. The wise invite correction, seek input, and surround themselves with people who aren't impressed by their title but are committed to their growth.

EVERY LEADER NEEDS A COUNSEL TABLE

Think of your leadership like sitting at the head of a table. The decisions you make impact real people—your family, your team, your legacy. So who's sitting at your counsel table?

You need:

- **Truth-Tellers**—People who love you enough to challenge your assumptions.
- **Veterans**—Those who've already walked through what you're walking into.
- **Spiritual Guides**—People anchored in the Word, whose advice isn't just smart, but godly.
- **Encouragers**—Those who remind you who you are when doubt creeps in.
- **Intercessors**—People who pray for you, not just talk to you.

These are the people who can say, "I don't think that's wise," or "Have you prayed about that?" and you'll actually listen. Because you trust their character, their track record, and their alignment with God's truth.

COUNSEL IS NOT CONSENSUS

Be careful: Seeking wise counsel doesn't mean polling everyone around you until you find someone who agrees with your opinion. That's not counsel—that's crowd-pleasing.

True counsel sometimes disagrees with you. It stretches you. It may even offend your ego. But it always protects your purpose. Godly counsel won't always affirm your feelings, but it will always guard your future.

> *Wounds from a friend can be trusted, but an*
> *enemy multiplies kisses.*
>
> —PROVERBS 27:6 (NIV)

If you're the smartest voice in your circle, you're in the wrong circle.

JESUS SOUGHT COUNSEL TOO

Even Jesus, before facing the cross, didn't isolate. He invited Peter, James, and John into the garden at Gethsemane to pray with Him. He didn't *need* their wisdom—He was wisdom incarnate—but He modeled relational transparency under pressure.

If Jesus surrounded Himself with trusted friends during His most agonizing moment, how much more should we?

LEADERSHIP INSIGHT: COUNSEL BUILDS CONFIDENCE

Seeking counsel doesn't make you weak—it makes you wise. Leaders who listen well lead well. Counsel brings clarity, checks ego, and strengthens resolve. It may slow down your decisions, but it will save you from costly mistakes, relational fallout, and spiritual drift.

You don't need more certainty—you need more clarity, and clarity often comes through the voices of people who see what you can't.

RELATIONSHIPS RUN THE WORLD

The most valuable currency in leadership is relationships. Titles may open doors, but trust opens hearts. Results may come and go, but relationships are what make impact last.

You want to build a great company? Start with great relationships.

You want to raise a strong family? Build it on trust, consistency, and love.

You want to change the world? Do it one intentional conversation at a time.

Because people follow those they trust, not just those in charge.

Leadership rises and falls on relationships. Behind every movement, every mission, every legacy, you'll find people who chose to invest in people. You'll find mentors who chose to pour in. Friends who stayed faithful. Coaches who believed when it wasn't popular. Leaders who walked closely instead of leading distantly.

You want to lead well? Learn to love well. Because at the end of the day, relationships don't just support your leadership. They are your leadership.

Key Highlights

- True influence isn't about titles or strategy—it's built through trust, connection, and consistent investment in people.
- Legacy is who you build, not what you build. Your greatest impact will often be measured in people, not accomplishments—those you mentor, love, and raise up.
- Great relationships take time, consistency, humility, and presence; they don't happen by accident.
- Audit your inner circle. Regularly evaluate who's sharpening, draining, or needing more or less of your time; proximity shapes your direction and capacity.
- Wise counsel multiplies your leadership. Strong leaders seek godly, honest voices around them—not yes-men, but truth-tellers who guard their growth and purpose.

Reflection Questions

1. Who in my life or leadership circle feels seen, valued, and prioritized by me right now—and who might feel overlooked? What's one relationship I've unintentionally neglected that needs renewed intentionality?
2. In what ways do I lead differently at work than I do at home? Where do I need to align my leadership values across both spheres? Do my actions reflect that I value people over performance in both spaces?
3. Do I focus more on ROI (Return on Investment) or ROR (Return on Relationships)? What relational investments am I making today that will yield long-term influence and legacy?

CHAPTER 11

LEADERS CREATE LEADERS

Before you are a leader, success is all about growing yourself. When you become a leader, success is all about growing others.

—JACK WELCH

The true test of leadership isn't how many people follow you. It's how many leaders you develop. Great leadership doesn't end with you; it begins with what you build in others. This chapter is about the kind of leadership that multiplies, not just manages. It's about moving from being the hero to becoming the guide. From center stage to the wings. From legacy as something you leave to legacy as someone you raise.

We live in a culture that celebrates the solo genius, the visionary who builds an empire on their back. But history, and heaven, are not impressed by what we build alone. They honor what we build *into others*. The most impactful leaders aren't those who die with the most followers, but those whose impact lives on through generations of leaders they've created.

The Bible is filled with this truth. In 2 Timothy 2:2 (NIV), Paul writes to Timothy, "And the things you have heard me say in the presence of many witnesses entrust to reliable people who will also be qualified to teach others." That's four generations of leaders in one sentence. Paul understood that real leadership is a chain reaction. Jesus modeled the same. He invested his time in 12 men who would change the world. He called them not to simply follow Him, but to become fishers of men. Leaders. Disciple-makers.

You see this multiplication mindset again in Exodus 18, when Moses is burning out trying to lead alone. His father-in-law, Jethro, gives him this counsel: "Select capable men from all the people ... and appoint them as officials" (verse 21 NIV). Moses was trying to carry the weight of leadership alone, but Jethro pointed him toward the principle of leadership delegation and distribution. One man's strength can inspire, but it's a team of leaders that builds a nation.

This idea isn't limited to Scripture—it's echoed in every generation of history-making leadership. Take John Wooden, the legendary UCLA basketball coach. He didn't just win championships; he developed men. His former players speak of how he shaped their character, taught them integrity, and prepared them to lead their families and communities. Wooden's greatness wasn't just the banners that hung in Pauley Pavilion—it was in the leaders who walked out of his locker room and into life with courage and conviction.

Leadership multiplication is also the secret to sustained growth in business. When Howard Schultz scaled Starbucks, he didn't micromanage every location. He built systems and, more importantly, leaders. He empowered others to carry the culture, make decisions, and lead from the front lines. Similarly, Craig Groeschel of Life. Church is known not just for building a megachurch but also for building a *leadership factory*. His focus isn't just to grow attenders but also to grow leaders who go out and lead well.

The problem is, many leaders are insecure. They hold onto authority like a possession, fearing that if they empower someone else, they'll become irrelevant. But in fact, the opposite is true. When you create other leaders, you expand your influence, not shrink it. You deepen your legacy, not dilute it. You honor God by stewarding your influence for the sake of others, not for the sake of your ego.

Simon Sinek once said, "Leadership is not about being in charge. It is about taking care of those in your charge." That kind of leadership is sacrificial. It stretches others. It lets them take risks and even fail, while you stand beside them as a coach, not a critic. It's not about creating clones—it's about cultivating character. It's not about getting credit—it's about giving people courage.

PRACTICAL LEADERSHIP STRATEGIES FOR CREATING LEADERS

IDENTIFY POTENTIAL EARLY

Leadership multiplication starts with identifying potential early. It's easy to spot polished leaders—those with presence, charisma, and a proven track record. But the best leaders don't just *spot* leaders; they *develop* them. And that development begins by seeing what others miss.

Not everyone who leads looks like a leader yet. Potential is often quiet. It may show up as someone who's always early, always serving, always asking questions. It may be the intern who takes notes when no one asks them to, or the team member who stays after a meeting to help carry the load. Leadership doesn't always walk in with a loud voice—it often grows from a quiet heart of responsibility and a posture of learning.

When you're evaluating who to invest in, don't look first for confidence first. Look for character. Look for humility—a willingness to be coached. Look for initiative—someone who doesn't wait to be told what needs to be done but steps in to meet a need. And look for hunger—that deep, internal drive to grow, to serve, to take on more than what's required. These are the seeds of greatness. These are the roots of a leader.

Jesus modeled this principle when He chose His disciples. He didn't go to the elite religious schools or the halls of political power. He found fishermen, a tax collector, ordinary men with very little to their name—but hearts that were teachable and lives He could mold. He looked past their current skill level and saw their future influence. He called out leadership in people before they even saw it in themselves.

You're not looking for the finished product—you're looking for *raw material*. And raw material has rough edges. It's messy. It needs time, coaching, and sometimes correction. But when you commit to seeing beyond where someone is to where they could be, you begin to lead like Jesus. You begin to multiply.

As a leader, part of your calling is to be a *talent scout*—someone who develops an eye for dormant potential. Like a great coach who spots the high school athlete that no one is recruiting, you must be willing to invest early and consistently. Often, the people with the highest ceilings are overlooked because they don't yet believe in themselves. Your belief in them becomes the spark. Your voice becomes the catalyst.

Remember this: The harvest always starts as seed. If you wait to invest until someone looks like a leader, you've missed the moment. Start early. Start small. Call out what you see. Water it with encouragement. Cultivate it with opportunity. And in time, you'll witness the incredible transformation of someone stepping fully into their calling—not just because they were ready, but because *you* were watching.

GIVE REAL RESPONSIBILITY

Once you've identified potential, the next step is to give real responsibility. This is where many leaders hesitate. It feels risky. After all, it's faster to just do it yourself. It's safer to keep control. But safe leadership never multiplies—it maintains. If you want to build leaders, you have to release control. You have to trust them with more than tasks. You have to entrust them with *ownership*.

There's a big difference between delegation and empowerment. Delegation says, *"Here's what to do—just get it done."* Empowerment says, *"Here's what we're building—own a piece of it."* One creates followers; the other creates leaders. Leaders aren't made in the shallow end. They're made in deep water—when they're asked to carry vision, to take the lead, to bear the weight of real decisions and live with the consequences.

Give your emerging leaders the space to lead meetings. Let them speak for the team. Let them own the outcome of a project from start to finish. Invite them into rooms they haven't been in before. Let them wrestle with strategy, not just execution. Will they make mistakes? Absolutely. That's the point. Growth doesn't come from perfection—it comes from pressure and reflection.

Think of the disciples again. Jesus didn't just teach His followers— He sent them out. He gave them authority to preach, to heal, to cast out demons (Luke 9:1–2). He didn't say, "Watch me for three years, and then, we'll see." He said, "You go. I'll guide you. But you *go*." That's what real responsibility looks like—it's developmental, not just directional. Jesus gave them space to try, to struggle, and to succeed.

In the same way, the leaders you're raising will never rise if they're only ever executing someone else's playbook. They need opportunities to lead where the outcomes *matter*. It may mean assigning them to manage a client relationship, lead a team meeting, or architect a new strategy. Whatever the situation, the key is this: They must feel the *weight* of leadership. Without that weight, they will never develop the strength to carry it.

This kind of responsibility builds confidence, decisiveness, and clarity. It forces someone to stop asking, "What do you want me to do?" and start asking, "What needs to be done?" That mindset shift— from obedience to ownership—is where real leadership begins.

But don't just throw people into the deep end and walk away. Come alongside them. Offer guidance, feedback, and support. Don't micromanage the how—coach the *why*. Let them bring their personality and style into the process. They may do it differently than you would. That's okay. That's healthy. It means they're growing into their own voice as a leader.

If you're going to create leaders, you have to give them real things to lead. That means risk. That means trust. That means release. But it's the only way to build something bigger than yourself. Give them the keys. Let them drive. That's how leaders are born.

MODEL, MENTOR, MULTIPLY

Leadership multiplication isn't just a strategy—it's a rhythm. And the rhythm is simple: Model, mentor, multiply. These three movements form the heartbeat of leadership development. Skip one, and the process breaks down. But walk through them with consistency and conviction, and you'll create leaders who don't just mimic you—they surpass you.

Modeling comes first. You can't teach what you haven't lived. People will only go as deep as the authenticity of your example. That's why great leaders don't lead from a pedestal—they lead from proximity. Leadership isn't taught in lectures—it's caught in everyday moments. Bring your developing leaders close enough to observe your life. Let them see your habits, your mindset, your prayer life, your discipline, your integrity under pressure. Let them see not just your public wins but your private disciplines too.

Let them see how you prepare for meetings. How you handle tension. How you make decisions when the answer isn't clear. How you apologize when you blow it. That kind of transparency isn't weakness—it's mentorship at its finest. When your team sees you wrestle with fear and still choose courage, they learn what real leadership looks like. When they hear you speak life over someone who made a mistake, they learn the power of grace under pressure. You are modeling not just leadership practices but leadership *spirit*, as well.

Mentoring follows naturally. Mentorship is not simply having coffee once a quarter and giving vague encouragement. It's *intentional*, *ongoing,* and *honest.* It requires creating space for feedback, questions, and conversations that go beneath the surface. Ask people what they're learning. Challenge them where they're comfortable. Speak to their blind spots—not to shame them, but to sharpen them.

Think of Jesus again. He didn't just preach sermons—He asked questions. He pulled His disciples aside after the crowds had gone and explained the deeper truths. He challenged Peter when his ego got in the way. He restored him when his failure overwhelmed him. Jesus mentored through proximity, patience, and purposeful correction.

You can do the same. Review decisions with your emerging leaders and ask them *why* they did what they did. Talk through mistakes with compassion and clarity. Share your own lessons. Invite them to give *you* feedback too—because great mentors are humble enough to keep growing themselves. Mentorship isn't about cloning yourself—it's about unlocking others' design and helping them become who they were made to be.

And finally, **multiply**. At some point, you have to let them go. *Release them.* This is where many leaders hesitate. You've walked with them. You've coached them. You've helped shape them—and now, it's time to *trust them.* Let them lead. Let them run. They will carry your DNA, but they'll also bring their own innovation, voice, and leadership flavor.

This is the moment where leadership becomes legacy. When you release a leader to walk in their calling, you are sending a ripple into the future. You're saying, "What God did through me, He can now do through you." And if you've modeled well and mentored consistently, the multiplication will take care of itself.

Because the leader you've raised won't just serve—they'll *start multiplying.* They'll begin to model, mentor, and multiply others. And that's when the true compounding of leadership happens. That's when you stop building an organization and start building a *movement.*

Model. Mentor. Multiply. It's not flashy. It's not fast. But it's how legacies are made.

CELEBRATE OTHERS' WINS PUBLICLY

This may seem simple—almost too simple to matter—but it's one of the most powerful tools in your leadership toolkit. Encouragement is not fluff; it's fuel. When used intentionally, it becomes a multiplier of confidence, clarity, and culture. And when it comes to building leaders, you cannot afford to withhold it.

A key part of developing leaders is *recognizing* their growth when it shows. Most people carry silent doubts. They wonder if they're doing it right. If they're making an impact. If they're even cut out for leadership. When a seasoned leader sees something in them—and then, *says it out loud*—it doesn't just affirm performance. It activates potential. It says, "I see you. I believe in you. You're stepping into who you were created to be."

And when that affirmation happens publicly, the effect is exponential. Private encouragement builds trust. *Public encouragement builds culture.* It communicates to your team that wins are noticed, that growth is celebrated, and that leadership is not a competition—it's a community.

Think about Jesus with Peter. After the resurrection, Jesus doesn't just privately restore Peter from his failure—He speaks vision over him:

Jesus said, "Simon son of John, do you love me?"
He answered, "Yes, Lord, you know that I love you."
Jesus said, "Take care of my sheep." John 21:16 (NIV)

Jesus affirmed Peter's calling *in front of the others*. That public declaration turned a shaky, impulsive disciple into a bold, foundational leader. That's the power of celebrating a win, even when it's still wrapped in process.

Celebrating others also kills pride and insecurity in your own heart. It forces you to take the spotlight off yourself and shine it on someone else. It keeps your leadership from becoming self-centered. If you can't cheer for the leaders you're raising, you're not building legacy—you're building ego.

Make a habit of celebrating wins often and out loud. A word in a team meeting. A shout-out in front of peers. A handwritten note. A public "thank you" that's specific, not generic. Recognize what they did, how they did it, and why it mattered. And don't just celebrate outcomes—celebrate *character*. Celebrate courage, humility, faithfulness, effort, and growth. When people know they're seen for more than just results, they'll bring their *whole selves* to the mission.

One of the greatest gifts you can give a developing leader *is* a *moment*—a moment when they realize their work matters. When they hear someone they respect speak life over them in front of others. When the seeds of calling begin to bloom into confidence. These moments shape people. They stick. And they often become turning points in a leader's journey.

So be generous with your words. Be quick to affirm. Be intentional about who gets the spotlight. Because when you celebrate the leaders around you, you're not just recognizing what they've done— you're *releasing them to become more.*

TEACH THEM TO DEVELOP OTHERS

It's one thing to lead well. It's another to raise up leaders. But the highest level of leadership—the kind that multiplies beyond your lifetime—is to *raise leaders who raise leaders.* This is where your impact doesn't just grow—it *compounds.* It spreads. It echoes through generations. It becomes a legacy in motion.

Too many leaders stop short. They pour into others, but they never teach them how to *do the same.* They create high-performing team members, but not *multipliers.* And in doing so, they build an impressive organization—but not a lasting one.

Again, think about what Paul wrote to Timothy in 2 Timothy 2:2 (NIV):

And the things you have heard me say in the presence of many witnesses entrust to reliable people who will also be qualified to teach others.

That's not just leadership—that's *generational* leadership. Paul was intentional not just about mentoring Timothy but also about teaching Timothy to *mentor others* who would, in turn, teach even more. That's the biblical blueprint. That's the ripple effect.

If you want to build something that outlives you, you must develop leaders with a multiplication mindset. Don't just ask your emerging leaders to grow in their own roles—challenge them to *look for the next wave.* Help them learn how to spot potential. Equip them to mentor. Show them how to pass on what they've been given. Make multiplication part of the expectation, not just the bonus.

Teach them to ask different questions:

- *Who am I developing right now?*
- *Who on my team needs to be challenged to lead?*
- *Who's showing signs of growth, initiative, and character?*
- *How can I create opportunities for them to lead?*

This is how culture is built. When everyone is looking for who to empower next, you've moved from addition to multiplication. You're no longer a bottleneck. You've created a system of ongoing leadership development—and that's what sustains a vision beyond a single person or generation.

And here's the beauty: When your leaders begin to pour into others, *they grow too.* Teaching deepens understanding. Coaching sharpens clarity. Mentoring forces you to embody what you say you believe. Everyone in the chain becomes stronger.

This is how movements start. Not with one charismatic leader at the center, but with hundreds of leaders carrying the same DNA, the same values, the same mission—because someone had the foresight to say, *"It's not about me—it's about who comes next."*

When Jesus gave the Great Commission in Matthew 28, He didn't say, "Go and gather followers." He said, "Go and make disciples" (verse 19 NIV). That meant making people who would make more disciples—people who would carry the mission forward, generation after generation. Jesus wasn't just multiplying ministry—He was multiplying *multipliers.*

So let me ask you: Are you building people who can build others? Are you teaching your leaders not just how to lead—but how to lead *leaders?*

Because that's the shift from leadership to legacy.

That's the shift from success to significance.

That's how leaders create *movements*—not just momentum.

Teach them to develop others. That's leadership done right.

Leadership is not a destination—it's a legacy. And legacy doesn't come from how many people follow you. It comes from how many people *lead* because of you. If your leadership ends with your own influence, then it ends too soon. But if your leadership multiplies—if it grows in the hands and hearts of others—then it lives on long after you're gone.

This is what separates managers from multipliers, bosses from builders, influencers from *impact-makers.* Leaders who create leaders are playing the long game. They're investing in eternity. They're not building monuments—they're building movements. And movements are never built alone.

We've seen it clearly: Jesus modeled it. Paul passed it down. Moses was taught it. World-changers like John Wooden and Craig Groeschel lived it. And now—you're called to *carry it.* You're not just called to lead—you're called to *reproduce leadership* in others. That means spotting potential before it's obvious, giving others real authority, modeling the way through your life, mentoring with patience and truth, celebrating progress, and teaching those you lead to lead others.

It's not about control—it's about commissioning. It's not about preserving power—it's about passing it on. That's the difference between a good leader and a great one. A good leader builds something worthwhile. A great one builds someone who can build something greater.

So as you lead—at home, in business, in ministry, in your community—ask yourself:

- Who am I raising up?
- Who have I empowered lately?
- Who will still be leading when I'm no longer in the room?

The answers to those questions will define the scope of your leadership and your legacy.

Because the ultimate aim of leadership isn't just influence—it's inheritance. It's leaving behind not just what you built, but *who* you built.

Leaders create leaders.

And leaders who create leaders?

They change the world.

Key Highlights

- True leadership isn't measured by how many people follow you, but by how many leaders you develop. Legacy begins when you move from being the hero to becoming the guide—building others, not just building things.
- Great leaders identify potential before it's fully formed. They look for character, humility, initiative, and hunger—not just confidence. Like Jesus and Paul, they invest in the raw material of future leaders.
- Delegation gives tasks, but empowerment gives ownership. To develop leaders, you must release control and let others lead—even if it means risk, mistakes, and growing pains. Responsibility is what builds leadership strength.
- Leadership development follows a rhythm: model authentic leadership, mentor with intentionality, and then, release others to multiply. This cycle creates leaders who surpass you—not just replicate you.
- The highest level of leadership is generational—raising leaders who raise others. That's when leadership becomes legacy. It's not about growing your influence—it's about growing others' capacity to lead without you.

Reflection Questions

1. Do I believe that leadership is about creating other leaders—not just gaining followers? How is that belief reflected in my current leadership approach?
2. Who around me shows quiet potential that I may have overlooked? How can I intentionally invest in them?
3. Am I entrusting others with real ownership—or just tasks?
4. What's one leadership opportunity I can release to someone else this week?

You Were Built to Lead

Trust in the LORD with all your heart, and do
not lean on your own understanding.

—Proverbs 3:5 (ESV)

When I first began down this path of writing, it almost felt fake. I had been journaling for nearly a decade and built the muscle of putting words on paper, but journaling for myself was different from writing something I intended to share with the world. Writing for an audience carries weight. It requires clarity, honesty, and the courage to put your heart in the open for others to see.

What I discovered in the process was that it forced me to wrestle deeply with the very truths I was writing about. I had to ask myself: *Would I teach this to my boys? Would I be proud if these words became part of their foundation for how they live and lead?* That question became my compass. And just like in leadership, once I committed to consistent, daily action, the process became more natural. Step by step, word by word, the vision turned into reality.

The principles of leadership we have explored throughout this book are more than skills or strategies. They are anchored in something greater than ourselves: a living relationship with God. If it weren't for starting each morning in Scripture, quieting my heart before Him, I don't believe this book would have ever come to life. That rhythm reminded me daily that you don't need the full road map to move forward. You just need enough faith to take the next step.

And then, in the midst of finishing this manuscript, the world was shaken. A young political activist and husband and father of two, Charlie Kirk, was shot and killed in front of the entire world while living out his calling—traveling to college campuses and engaging in open debate about cultural issues. I didn't follow Charlie closely, and I didn't know much about him before that tragic day. But with my being the same age as him, also raising young children, the news pierced me to my core.

His story brought into sharp focus the very lessons I had been writing about for months. You may not agree with all of his views or opinions, but there is no denying that he was a strong leader who lived with conviction. As I reflected on the cost of leadership, I realized I had never truly considered the ultimate cost: laying down your very life. That thought drove me back to the Gospels and to the ultimate example of leadership: Jesus Christ. He gave His life as the ultimate act of love and sacrifice for others.

Now, I am not comparing Charlie Kirk to Jesus. But his death served as a sobering reminder that we will all face the end of our days. The question is not *if* we will die, but *how* we will live until that day comes. Are we willing to embrace our calling even if it costs us everything?

That reality has reminded me just how fragile life truly is. How quickly our time can be cut short, and how urgent the call to lead really is. Leadership is not something we can postpone for "someday." None of us are guaranteed someday. All we have is today, and what we choose to do with it will echo long after we're gone.

We are living in a crucial time in history. A time when noise is louder than truth, when distraction is easier than discipline, when self-promotion is rewarded more than service. But it is also a time ripe for leaders. Leaders who are willing to stand firm in faith, to live by conviction instead of convenience, to guide their families, teams, and communities with courage and compassion.

This call is not reserved for the strong, the famous, or the well-positioned. It's for all of us. Men and women of every age, background, and story. The world doesn't need perfect leaders; it needs surrendered leaders. It needs people who are willing to take responsibility, love sacrificially, and live anchored to something greater than themselves.

So, wherever you are reading this, whether you're in a season of influence or obscurity, whether you're leading a company, raising a family, mentoring a teenager, serving in your church, or simply leading yourself, my prayer is that this book has encouraged you to step up and step out in your call to lead.

Lead with love in motion.
Lead with faith over fear.
Lead not to be impressive, but to make an eternal impact.
You were built to lead.

Acknowledgments

This book would not have been possible without the people who have stood by me, encouraged me, and pushed me to keep going when the road was long.

First and foremost, to my wife, Peyton—you are my rock, my greatest supporter, and the one who has believed in me even when I doubted myself. To my boys, you are the reason I strive every day to build a life and a legacy worth passing on. You remind me what truly matters, and you inspire me to lead with love, courage, and vision.

To my mom, Elizabeth, thank you for your unwavering belief in me and for planting the seeds of faith, resilience, and hard work that have carried me this far.

To Kate Simmons, my assistant—your diligence, organization, and dedication have made this journey possible. You've taken on so much behind the scenes, and this book would not have come together without you.

To the team at Best Seller Publishing, thank you for your guidance, expertise, and commitment to excellence. You've helped turn this vision into a reality.

To my Sunchase team members, I am grateful for your hard work, loyalty, and shared belief in the mission we are building together. You are the foundation of what we've accomplished and what lies ahead.

To my business partners—Jeremy Johnson, Robert Rinke, and Rhys Rinke—thank you for your trust, your wisdom, and your willingness to dream big with me.

To my pastor and good friend, Nathan Pooley—thank you for your encouragement to share my faith within my business and the world. Your guidance has reminded me to keep my eyes fixed on what truly matters as I seek to lead with faith and integrity.

To my coach, Trevor McGregor—thank you for your support and wisdom and for challenging me to level up over the past few years. Truly, as iron sharpens iron, so one person sharpens another!

Finally, to all of you reading this—thank you for walking with me on this journey. This book is not just mine; it belongs to you as well.

Made in USA - Kendallville, IN
24484_9781969338588
12.29.2025 2110